TWINKLE SEWS

Copyright © 2009 by Wenlan Chia

Published in the United States by Potter Craft,
an imprint of the Crown Publishing Group,
a division of Random House, Inc., New York.
www.crownpublishing.com
www.pottercraft.com

POTTER CRAFT and colophon is a registered
trademark of Random House, Inc.

Library of Congress Cataloging-in-
Publication Data
Chia, Wenlan.
  Twinkle sews : 25 handmade fashions from the runway to your
wardrobe / Wenlan Chia.
    p.   cm.
  Includes index.
  ISBN 978-0-307-40935-5
  1. Clothing and dress.   2. Sewing   I. Title
  TT515.C493   2009
  646'.3—dc22   2009001504
Printed in China

Design by La Tricia Watford
Fashion Photography by Kevin O'Brien
Still Photography by Michael Crouser
Hair by David Cruz for Redken
Makeup by Chantel Miller for M.A.C.
Nails by Indigo Smith for CND
Models: Kate Canestri and Diana Sillaots
Writer: Nadine Rubin
Pattern Writer: Carole Ann Camp
Pattern Assistants: Yuki Sekiya and Emma Walkerdine

10 9 8 7 6 5 4 3 2 1

First Edition

TWINKLE SEWS

25 HANDMADE FASHIONS FROM THE RUNWAY TO YOUR WARDROBE

WENLAN CHIA

POTTER
CRAFT

NEW YORK

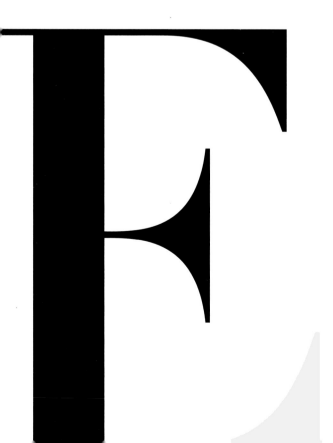
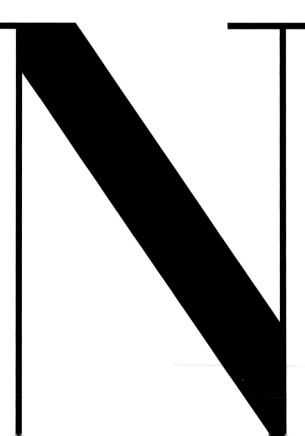

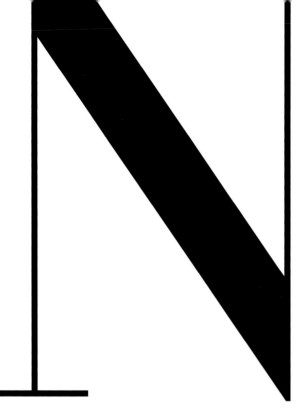
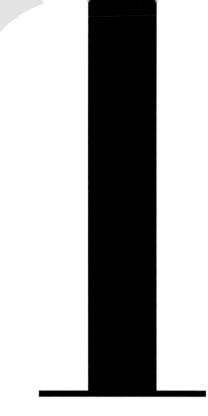

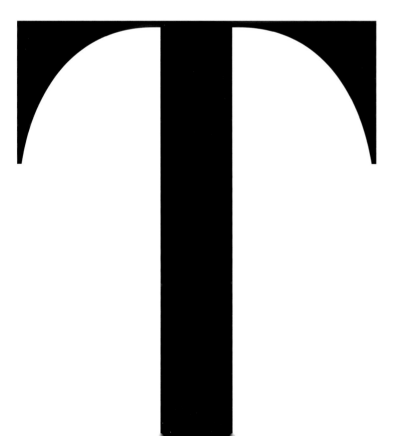

INTRODUCTION

Open your eyes to inspiration.

The first step to becoming a creative sewer is opening your eyes to inspiration. I do that each season when I create my Twinkle by Wenlan collection. And each season, my designs need to jibe with the key trends. To do this, I mix the playful spirit that my designs have become known for with silhouettes that run the gamut from girlie to glamorous. But at the same time, my customers can wear a Twinkle piece for years. Thanks to the many unique touches that I have worked hard to create, I'm told that my clothes have the lifespan of a classic, albeit a quirky one.

You know a Twinkle piece when you see one: young, fresh, whimsical. There's a downtown sensibility, an eccentric glamour, and a playful sophistication. I mix colors and patterns that might ordinarily seem at odds—a purple scarf with a brown floral skirt, or cream and black stripes with tweed. My skirts, cut slim, on the bias, or with an A-line flare, are done in sassy colors like red or turquoise and paired with soft, floaty tops. I add flourishes such as ruffled hemlines or pleats that take their cue from Japanese origami. I combine the dressy and the casual—a raw-edged silk camisole with cotton shorts, or a houndstooth skirt with a contrasting sweater. For even greater contrast, I mix soft, airy fabrics, like satin or lace, with pinstripes.

My signature looks include custom prints and original designs based on imagery I cull from the arts, my travels around the world, and even my daydreams. I find inspiration for my designs all around me: I was thinking about the curlicues in nineteenth-century ironwork when I designed the soft curves of a pretty keyhole neckline; mod pocket details have their roots in a vintage jacket I found at a downtown flea market. There's a bit of a vintage vibe, discernible in echoes of the forties and the sixties, but when I work with bygone eras, I try to make sure the design stays fresh and girlish. There's the occasional nod to boho and nautical and a couple of looks borrowed from the boys.

My designs never lose their youthful spirit: My collection is worn by Japanese teenagers and forty-year-old New York women alike.

I always made clothes for myself when I was growing up, and I never lost my love for sewing or for teaching others how to sew like I can, which brings us to this book. With it, I inspire you to look at the world the way a fashion designer does, and let your imagination go free. If you follow the easy-to-use instructions for each project, you will be able to bring Twinkle's whimsical take on fashion to life. Each project or styling tip is based on one of my unique runway designs. The key shapes are relaxed and easy on the body: loose-waisted shifts, tunics, skirts, tops, and the occasional long dress. The tops and dresses all contain Twinkle's signature drop-shoulder sleeves, raglan sleeves, or spaghetti straps.

For this book, I was inspired by the popularity of *Project Runway*, but I take it a step further. Instead of just watching other designers make their own projects, you will learn how to bring a fashionable edge into your own home-sewn projects. I will show you how to create something basic that you will be proud to wear. You don't have to be a couture seamstress to complete these garments; the projects are innovative but not too challenging. The techniques are not difficult, but the design and the way I play with fabric add a fashionable edge.

Every project in the book contains clear instructions to direct you from choosing fabric to cutting and sewing. Patterns for each garment come in five sizes—0, 4, 8, 12, and 16—on the disc accompanying the book. The patterns are in PDF and Adobe Illustrator format and can be printed on 8½" x 11" (21.5cm x 28cm) sheets on your home printer. Tape the sheets together, matching the numbers on each corner, and then cut out the pattern pieces. The clear markings on the patterns make taping and cutting them easy to manage from home.

Having published three modern knitting books, I have gleaned from my readers that learning design, craft, and creativity through books can be rewarding and inspiring. In many ways, though, sewing is more customizable than knitting. As a sewer, you can whip up a simple skirt or top and try it on right away to find out if it works. Once you've tweaked it and have a perfect fit, you have a template for your future projects that you know in advance will work. In this book, you will learn enough to master the seams, darts, zippers, and buttons that are necessary to make a basic wardrobe. You will also learn about the differences between the various fabrics available to the home sewer and the wisdom of spending a little more for better materials. I will teach you how to properly preshrink and prepare fabric and how to pick the right fabric for each project. In addition, you'll find extra advice in the Twinkle Tips scattered throughout. However, the real fun is using these basic skills to add a unique, fashion-conscious touch to your wardrobe. I encourage you to explore color, materials, and notions for a unique garment. I will show you how to mix and match different fabrics in one project, and then how to duplicate the idea in another dress. As you become more adept at finishing these projects, I invite you to make your own changes to my patterns. That menswear-inspired top you love? I'll show you how to lengthen it so that you have a dress too. The possibilities are as limitless as your imagination.

Project by project, this book offers Twinkle fans more of what they adore. It is not an A to Z of home sewing but a guide to get you stitching, unleash your creativity in fabric, and bring your fashion dreams to life!

TWINKLE TECHNIQUES

We are living in a time of endless possibility and creativity when it comes to fashion. While some sewing techniques remain constant—a seam is a seam the world over—how you sew the seam is entirely up to you. In this section, I describe some of the choices you have for making all the garments in this book. Remember, you are creating a garment for yourself. Don't be afraid to select a different fabric or color from those I suggest. Topstitching, buttons, bows, beads, rivets, ribbons, trims, and lace are only a few ways to embellish your garment. I've made some suggestions, but I encourage you to be creative and do your own thing.

USING THE PATTERNS

I have used the word *self* on the patterns to indicate the main or primary fabric for the garment, and the word *combo* to indicate contrasting fabrics and trims. Sometimes, there may be several different combos, or contrasting fabrics, in one garment. In these cases the different contrasting fabrics will be numbered combo 1, combo 2, etc. Where interfacing is needed, *fusible* is indicated on the pattern. Lined garments will include lining pattern pieces as well. Each pattern piece indicates how many pieces should be cut and of which fabric.

When preparing to make a garment from the book, first choose your size, and print out the pattern on your home printer using letter-size 8½" x 11" (21.5cm x 28cm) paper. Tape the pieces of paper together into a grid, matching the circle and number on each corner, and then cut out the pattern pieces. Before cutting the fabric, double-check what fabric you'll be using for each pattern piece. The symbol chart at right explains all pattern markings, such as darts, shirring, pleats, topstitching, buttons, button-holes, zippers, and elastic. Before cutting and sewing, read through the sewing instructions, checking every detail on the patterns to conceptualize the process of making the garment.

The first page of each project pattern contains a diagram of the pattern pieces. This is not a cutting diagram, but rather is designed to show all of the pieces used in the garment. The diagram key explains which pieces, and how many, to cut from which fabric. The yardage amounts provided for each pattern work with either 45" (114cm) or 60" (1.5m) widths of fabric and for all the sizes. You will need to lay out the pattern pieces on the corresponding fabrics and fit them on the fabric however works for you, remembering to watch the grain lines. If you want to be more precise and purchase the exact amount of fabric needed, lay out the pattern in your size to both 45" (114cm) and 60" (1.5m) widths to determine the exact length of fabric needed.

The patterns are not designed to be cut on the fold of the fabric; they were made to be cut on a flat piece of fabric. Instead of providing half of the front and back, to be cut on the fold, the entire front and back pattern pieces are given. Note: Because you are using only one layer of fabric, it is important to remember when cutting the sleeves, or any other piece needing a left and a right, to place the pattern piece right side (text side) up for one sleeve and right side down for the other sleeve. If you cut two with the pattern piece right side up, you will end up with two right sleeves!

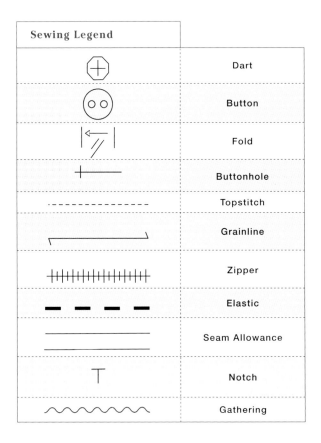

Sewing Legend	
	Dart
	Button
	Fold
	Buttonhole
	Topstitch
	Grainline
	Zipper
	Elastic
	Seam Allowance
	Notch
	Gathering

SIZING

There is no one pattern that fits every woman on the planet perfectly. All printed patterns are approximations. In this book, I offer suggestions as to size, but you will have to adjust the patterns to fit you.

I HAVE INCLUDED PATTERNS FOR FIVE SIZES: 0, 4, 8, 12, and 16. Generally, there is a 2" (5cm) difference between sizes in the chest, waist, and hip circumference. If you are between sizes, print out the patterns for both sizes, lay the smaller size pattern on top of the larger size, and draw a middle line on the larger pattern to create a size in between.

To find your size for skirts, measure your hips and add 2" (5cm) for seam allowances and 1" to 2" (2.5cm–5cm) for ease. Look up the resulting number on the chart on the following page and choose the pattern that comes closest (this is an approximation); it is easier to adjust the waist by changing the side seam, the widths of the darts, or the amount of gathering than it is to change the hip size. Try the simplest skirt with some scrap fabric and adjust the size accordingly. Use this size as a guide for the other skirts in the skirts chapter. For an easy way to find your exact skirt measurements, choose a straight skirt from your closet that fits you perfectly. Measure the hips (or the widest part) and the waist. Add 2" (5cm) for seam allowances. Find these numbers in the chart on the following page.

Size Chart					
Body Measurement	Size 0	4	8	12	16
Bust	32" (81cm)	34" (86cm)	36" (91cm)	38" (96.5cm)	40" (101.5cm)
Waist	26" (66cm)	28" (71cm)	30" (76cm)	32" (81cm)	34" (86cm)
Hips	35" (89cm)	37" (94cm)	39" (99cm)	41" (104cm)	43" (109cm)

The length of the skirt or garment is entirely up to you. I have shown only one length. Feel free to lengthen or shorten your skirt to fit your body shape and taste.

For tops and dresses with sleeves, measure your bust (don't take your bra size) and add 2" (5cm) for seam allowances and 3" to 5" (7.5cm–12.5cm) for ease. Look up this number up on the chart above and choose the corresponding pattern size. For most of the patterns, the width across the shoulders isn't too important. You will have to adjust these patterns to fit you. In most cases, it is better to err on the side of too large rather than too small. You can always take in the seam allowance or adjust the darts, pleats, or gathers. Most of the tops in this book are loose fitting and have raglan sleeves or drop shoulders, so exact fit in those isn't as important—the amount of ease is your call.

On the garments with bra-style tops, pick a size that you think will fit your bust and, using the pattern pieces for that size, make a mock-up of the cups out of scraps. Don't forget to keep the straight of the grain of the scrap lined up with the straight of the grain of the pattern. Having the give or stretch of the fabric going in the wrong direction can make a difference in how the bra fits. Try your cups on with and without your bra, depending on how you will eventually wear the garment. Make the cup to fit you. If you have to take in large seams, try a smaller size. If the cup is too small, try the larger size. Don't worry if our numbers don't match the size you think you are. And remember that your body may not be completely symmetric: Adjust each cup separately to fit your shape. If you have a favorite bra that fits perfectly but has seen better days, cut the cups out of the bra and use them as a pattern for the garment. Whatever adjustments you make, remember to also make them on the bra lining pieces.

Remember, do not go by what you think your size is. If you think you are a size 4 and measure yourself and find you need our size 6, go with our size 6. It is easier to adjust down than up.

FABRIC

Go to a fabric store and wander. Enjoy the vast array of colors and textures. Feel the fabrics. What attracts you? What do you think will feel good when you wear it? What fabric will make a statement about who you are? What fabric is just plain fun?

There are also some practical things to consider when selecting your fabric: Is it washable? How much will it shrink? Is it easy to sew? If you are new to sewing, choosing filmy chiffon, velvet, or soft silk might not be the best choice because they slide around while sewing and can be difficult to handle even for experienced sewers.

Be sure to read the care instructions on the end of the bolt. Find a fabric that matches your lifestyle: If you always throw your clothes into a washer and dryer and don't know where the dry cleaner is, don't select fabric that is labeled dry clean only! And if you choose a fabric that can be washed, be sure to preshrink it before you lay out the pattern.

DRAPE

How a fabric drapes is another consideration. Some fabrics, such as challis, chiffon, silk, and some rayons, flow and swirl around nicely and are great if you want a soft, flowing look, as found in the Carnival Dress (page 136) and Dark Secrets (page 96). Other fabrics, like duck cloth, drape like cardboard and are very stiff. Felt, for example, would not be a good choice for Cool Contrasts (page 62) or Budding Romance (page 66). Another consideration is how much cling you want. Some garments and bodies look great with a really clingy fabric, while others do not! When you are in the fabric store, don't be afraid to unroll a yard or two (1m–1.8m) from the bolt to see how the fabric drapes.

HINT: When you preshrink, try to use the same conditions, water temperature, and soap you will be using when you wash your garment.

NAP

Another consideration when purchasing fabric is nap. If you run your hand one way down the fabric, it feels smooth; if you run your hand the other way, it's rough. Many fabrics have nap—velvet is the most obvious. There are two reasons to check the nap of the fabric. First, it is a general rule that all pieces of a garment should have the nap going in the same direction from top to bottom or head to toe. Second, it may be necessary to purchase more fabric to accommodate laying out all the pattern pieces in the same direction. In general, it always is better to purchase too much fabric than not enough.

Another kind of nap or direction occurs on fabric with a one-way design. This is most noticeable in some patterned fabrics. If you choose a fabric with nap, you don't want some of the nap or pattern of the pieces in a garment to go in opposite directions. Or, on the other hand, maybe you do!

GRAIN

In most cases, pattern pieces are cut on the grain, or straight, of the fabric, which means that the vertical line of the garment piece is parallel to the selvage or edge of the fabric. Crosswise grain is perpendicular to the selvage. The arrows on each pattern piece show you how the grain of the garment should lay in relation to the selvage.

HINT: If you pull on the fabric on the grain with two hands about 6″ (15cm) apart, there will be very little give or stretch. But if you pull on the bias (the diagonal), there is considerable stretch. This is generally true unless, of course, you have chosen a double knit, which has stretch in all directions.

RIGHT SIDE/WRONG SIDE

If your fabric is the same on both sides, decide which side you want for the inside and mark a WS (for *wrong side*) in the seam allowance of all of the pieces. Traditionally, the inside of the garment, or the side closest to the body, was the wrong side, and the outside of the garment, or the side facing the public, was the right side. For some fabric, it's just a matter of taste, and you can decide which is the wrong side and which is the right side–these days there is no "wrong" side even if the designs are different on each side.

If the garment has many pieces, such as the Carnival Dress (page 136), or many similar pieces, such as the Flapper Camisole (page 130), write the number of the piece in the seam allowance. For extra assurance on some of the garments, mark the top and bottom. You'd be amazed at how easy it is to forget which end is up!

SEAMS

All seams are sewn right sides together, unless the directions for a specific garment suggest otherwise.
For decades, the standard seam allowance for most home-sewn fashions was ⅝″ (1.5cm). Today many people use a ½″ (13mm) allowance. Collars, facings, ties, and so on usually have ¼″ to ⅜″ (6mm–9.5mm) seam allowances. The seam allowance depends somewhat on the type of fabric and the way you want to finish the seam. If you are using a fabric that frays easily and you don't intend to finish the edges, plan on the ⅝″ (1.5cm) allowance.

If you have a serger, ⅜" or ½" (9.5mm or 13mm) seam allowances will work in most cases. Most of our patterns are designed with ⅜" or ½" (9.5mm or 13mm) allowances. If you choose a different size seam allowance, adjust the pattern pieces accordingly. If the pieces are not marked, assume ½" (13mm) seam allowance. The instructions will tell you when a different size seam allowance is needed.

After you have sewn the seam, "set" it by pressing the seam allowance open. On wools, don't forget to use a pressing cloth between the seam allowance and the garment. You don't want the lump or line of the seam allowance to show on the outside of the garment. Don't do this with velvet, however, unless you have a special tool for the express purpose of pressing velvet.

GRADING SEAMS

The allowance of some seams, such as those on collars, lapels, facings, and underarms, will need to be trimmed to reduce bulk and prevent ridges from showing on the garment's public side. Reducing any seam allowance is referred to as *trimming* (¼" [6mm] is the standard width). *Grading* is done by trimming the seam allowances to different widths: The seam closest to the public side is trimmed slightly wider than the one on the wrong side. Enclosed seams like those on collars, lapels, and cuffs are graded to give them sharp, turned edges. Trim the narrower side first, then trim the other side a little wider.

FINISHING SEAMS

Finishing a seam keeps many fabrics from fraying and keeps the inside of your garment looking tidy. If you plan to put a lining in your garment, finishing the seams isn't quite so important, unless the fabric frays easily. There are many ways to finish seams: Many of the seams in this book are finished with a serger. If you don't have a serger, you can zigzag close to the edge instead, or use pinking shears. Some sewing machines even have a "faux" serger stitch, which looks just like a serged edge.

I have used French seams on garments with seams that may show on the outside and those sewn from light or flimsy fabric. French seams are sewn first with the wrong

sides together, and then the seam is resewn with right sides together. The seam edges get encased into the second seam, which creates a nice, neat finish and also helps eliminate fraying.

Today there are a variety of glues and iron-on tapes for seam finishing. The glues can be used to keep an edge from fraying or to tack slippery seams together while you sew; iron-on seam tapes work similarly. One caution, though: Test the tape or glue in an inconspicuous place on your fabric first. When used to prevent fraying, some glues dry hard and in some cases have sharp points. These points scratch the skin and are very uncomfortable to wear. Also, some glues stiffen the fabric so much that you lose its flowing quality. However, glue works very well if you are putting in a regular zipper, since it eliminates the need for pins or basting.

STITCHING

Today's sewing machines come with a host of presser feet and fancy stitches. Even the least expensive machines have many different stitches. In my grandmother's day, the straight stitch was it. One could change the stitch length, and possibly backstitch. Then along came zigzagging. Now, with all of the computer technology available, the sewing machine can do unbelievable things our grandmothers never dreamed of. For regular stitching, use the recommended normal stitch length for your machine, or ten to twelve stitches per inch (2.5cm). Most machines indicate the "regular" stitch on the dial with a mark, dot, or color change.

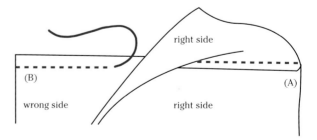

When making a French seam, first stitch the seam with wrong sides together (A). Then sew the seam with right sides together (B).

There will also be a "regular" presser foot, usually with two prongs. Sometimes the zigzag foot serves for both straight stitching and zigzagging. If you have a regular presser foot, use it. You may be tempted to use the zigzag foot for everything, but sometimes, especially with softer fabrics such as chiffon or silk, the fabric bunches up in the slot of the zigzag foot.

Basting Stitch

Basting stitches are straight and long, only a few stitches per inch (2.5cm). They are easy to remove, so they are great if you want to sew parts of your garment together to see if it fits. Basting stitches are also needed to ease a curved line to a straight line or when making ruffles. You also can baste by hand; then you can use really long stitches!

Zigzag Stitch

Zigzag stitches come in handy if you do not have a serger and want to finish the edges of your seams. Some machines do not have a buttonhole attachment and use the zigzag stitch to make the buttonhole. Be sure to use the zigzag presser foot when zigzagging, or you will break a lot of needles.

Backstitch

Most seams are backstitched at the beginning and end of a seam to keep the seam ends from coming apart. Read your machine's manual for directions on how to make your machine backstitch or stitch backward. You only need to take a few stitches back and forth.

Beware: On very soft fabrics, such as silk or chiffon, you run the risk of getting the fabric bunched up in the presser foot when you backstitch. Attaching stabilizer to the fabric can prevent this. There are a variety of stabilizers on the market. The basic categories are "tear-off," "cut-off," "wash-away," and "heat-disintegrating." Cut-off stabilizers are softer and work well on soft fabrics. Read the directions on the package to be sure that the stabilizer is appropriate for your fabric. To use, press a small strip of stabilizer in the seam allowance at the beginning and end of the seam. This will give the machine's feed dogs something to grab. Another solution is to skip the back stitch and use a little fabric glue on the end of the seam thread.

Topstitch

Topstitching is straight or regular stitching that is seen on the garment by choice, not hidden on the inside. Topstitching can be functional, decorative, or both. Functional topstitching usually holds facings and linings from showing on the right (public) side on different edges, such as the neck edge, while at the same time adding to the overall design of the garment. Many of the suggestions for topstitching in this book are very close to the edge. Some machines come with a presser foot that helps you sew a neat line of stitching amazingly close to the edge. If you have one, use it. If you don't have one, get one!

With all the fancy stitches available today, there is no reason to limit your topstitching options to the straight stitch. Experiment! Remember that topstitching shows, so choose the color of your thread to enhance the design of your garment.

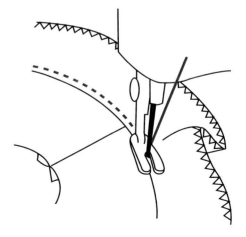

Using a sewing machine for topstitching.

Stay Stitch

Whenever you need to clip a curve or cut to a point, it is a good idea to stay stitch first. Stay stitching is a line of stitching that is sewn just to the right of the seam line in the seam allowance, as close as possible to the seam line but not on it. The stay stitches keep the fabric from "breaking through" the seam-line stitches.

Understitch

Understitching is mostly used to keep facings and linings from rolling to the outside and showing. It also helps to keep edges flatter. To understitch, clip curves and grade the seam if necessary. If the fabric is heavy, such as wool, grading the seam helps to eliminate bulk, but on lightweight fabrics, especially those that fray easily, it may be better to leave the full seam allowance. Move all of the seam allowances and the lining or facing to one side. Lay the garment to the left and the seam allowances and facing or lining to the right. To the right of the seam line and as close to the seam as possible, stitch the seam allowances and the lining or facing together. It helps to use a zipper foot.

Stitch in the Ditch

Quilters love stitching in the ditch. It is a way to sew on the right side of the fabric without the stitches showing—the opposite of topstitching. Basically, it is sewing on top of a seam that already exists. It is very useful for attaching waistbands and sewing some parts of linings to the garment from the right side.

Using a waistband as an example, press the seam allowance to the inside on one side of the waistband. Sew the unpressed edge of the waistband to the garment with right sides together. Finish the ends of the waistband, clip the corners, and fold the waistband with wrong sides together, tucking the pressed seam allowance to the inside. Place a few pins just to hold everything in place.

From the right side, pin in the seam line, or "ditch," making sure you catch the bottom folded edge of the waistband on the inside **(A)**.

When you sew, pull the first pin out, sew up to the point of the second pin, take the second pin out, and so on around the waist **(B)**. If you have pinned accurately and often, the inside bottom edge of the waistband should be neatly sewn to the skirt and the stitches do not show on the right side. Don't forget that you can always hand-sew the inside edge with slip stitches.

Hand Stitches

While most of the sewing in this book is done by machine, once in a while it is necessary to pick up a needle and do it by hand. Slip stitches, or blind stitches, are hand stitches used to tack something down without the stitches showing on the public/outside of the garment—a hem or facing, for example. These stitches are tiny, usually only catch one or two threads, are not pulled tight, and are barely seen if at all. Use a single thread of a matching color for these stitches.

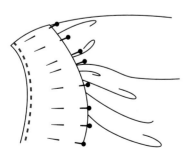

Stitch in the Ditch (A)

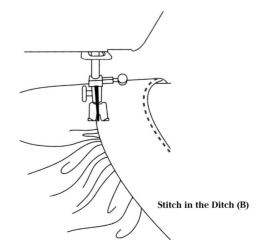

Stitch in the Ditch (B)

DARTS, PLEATS, AND GATHERS

Darts, pleats, and gathers are used to make a flat piece of fabric curve to fit around the human body. Most women need darts, pleats, or gathers around the bust, waist, hips, tummy, and derriere. They are almost always interchangeable; which one you choose is a design issue. Some of the fabric that needs to be taken in for a dart, pleat, or gather may be in a seam. For example, on a straight skirt, the hip "darts" are usually part of the side seam.

In garments with a princess line, the excess fabric resulting from shaping is eliminated in the princess seam of the bust, waist, and tummy. A princess line is an invisible line that runs vertically from either the shoulder, neckline, or armhole down through the apex (bust point). It is roughly located right in the middle of center front (or center back) and side seam. By creating a princess seam, shaping can be done without darts, pleats, or gathers, because all the excess fabric from shaping the bust and waist will be moved into the princess seam and eliminated.

In addition to regulating the shape and design of a garment, darts, pleats, and gathers also help change the size of different parts of the garment. If you have an hourglass shape, you may need more darts around the waist than a woman with an apple shape.

LININGS

Almost all of the garments in this book have linings. Linings, usually made from lightweight fabrics, give body to the garment, create a slight opacity for see-through fabrics, and give the inside of the garment a professional look. In addition, linings help finish some edges, such as necklines and waistlines, eliminating the need for facings. Depending on the fabric you select, you may or may not need a lining. However, on the balloon skirt in Next Big Thing (page 100), the lining is necessary to create the balloon effect. Jazz Hall (page 36) in the skirt chapter uses the lining to hold two of the four flounces.

To ensure that the lining does not hang below the skirt, pin the wrong side of the lining to the wrong side of the skirt before sewing the hem of the lining. Hang the garment so you can easily see the hem of the skirt. Pin the hem of the lining up so that it doesn't show below the bottom of the skirt.

TIP: To keep the lining from sliding around, crochet a 1" to 2" (2.5cm–5cm) long chain of sewing thread and tack one end of the chain to the seam allowance of the lining and the other end of the chain to the seam allowance of the garment.

ZIPPERS

The zipper, which came into fashion in the 1930s, is still considered a recent addition to clothing construction. Today there are many kinds of zippers. Some have metal teeth, some have plastic. Some are designed to be seen as part of the garment, while others are hidden and invisible. Most zipper closures in this book use invisible zippers, in which the stitching doesn't show on the public side, or the outside, of the garment. But choose the method that works best for you or the way you were taught. You may even want to skip the zipper and use buttons, snaps, hooks and eyes, or even hook and loop tape instead. **Note:** Invisible zippers require a special zipper foot available wherever zippers are sold.

Invisible zippers are usually put in before the seam is sewn. It is easy to get your tops and bottoms, lefts and rights, and insides and outsides confused when putting in an invisible zipper. Follow the directions on the package exactly. Mark the appropriate seam allowances with WS (for *wrong side*) before you cut out the pieces. If you feel more secure using a regular zipper, go for it; just follow the directions on the package, which usually includes sewing the seam before you put in the zipper. In the directions for each garment, I have suggested when to put in the zipper.

HINT: If you are not putting in an invisible zipper, this is where fabric glue really comes in handy. Just glue the seam allowance to the zipper tape and sew. Try not to get too much glue on the stitching line. Some glues gum up your needle, which in turn sticks to the thread, which then gets tangled up in a gigantic knot. Not fun!

BUTTONS AND BUTTONHOLES

Buttons are both functional and decorative and provide you with an opportunity for creativity. In Take Manhattan (page 70) and On the Sidelines (page 64), I have used rivets as a decorative addition. If you do not have a rivet-attaching machine, find and use some funky buttons instead.

Many of the garments in this book have buttonholes, some for buttons and some for ties. Every sewing machine makes buttonholes, but each machine has its own unique attachments and methods. Follow the directions that came with your machine or use your own creative method.

BIAS TAPE

Purchased bias tape comes in a variety of colors, a few different widths, and two basic styles: single- and double-fold. Single-fold is often used on neck and armhole edges as a seam finishing. The tape does not show on the right side of the garment, but one row of stitching does show and acts as topstitching. Double-fold tape slips over the edge and is sewn very close to the edge of the tape. The tape shows, as does the stitching.

If you look at double-fold bias tape, you'll notice that the two edges don't quite match up. There is a reason for this. Lay the tape over the edge with the shorter side to the outside of the garment, the longer to the inside. Working on the right side of the garment, stitch close to the edge of the tape. If all works out well, the longer underside of the bias tape should be caught in the stitching. This doesn't work as well on very bulky fabrics, because there is too much fabric to cover, and the longer back side gets pulled up. If you make your own bias tape, you can make the tape wider and also a little longer on the back side.

Making and Attaching Bias Tape

Despite the many colors of bias tape available, it seems as if you can never find the exact color you need. The solution, of course, is to make your own. Another advantage to making your own is that you can make the tape the exact length and width you want.

Single-Fold Bias Tape

To make your own single-fold bias tape, cut a strip on the bias ½" (13mm) wider than you want the finished tape to be. (Cutting the bias strips 1" [2.5cm] wide is the norm for most garments.) Press under ¼" (6mm) along each long edge.

With right sides together, pin so that the fold of the tape is ½" (13mm) from the edge of the garment. Sew on the fold line. Clip the curves and understitch. Press the tape to the inside of the garment. Topstitch the bias tape to the garment from the right side. The distance from the edge of the garment to the topstitching should catch the bias tape on the inside, approximately ⅜" (9.5mm).

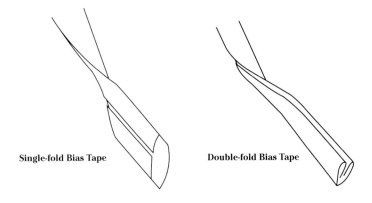

Single-fold Bias Tape   **Double-fold Bias Tape**

Double-Fold Bias Tape

To make your own double-fold bias tape, cut the tape on the bias ½" (13mm) wider than you want the finished tape to be. Fold the tape in half lengthwise with wrong sides together and press. Fold and press both edges of the tape to the center fold. Consider making one of these folds so that it comes just short of the center fold line. This will make one of the folds a tiny bit larger. Press the center fold again.

Stay stitch or baste the facing or lining to the garment using a ¼" (6mm) seam allowance. Clip the curves. The raw edge of the garment should fit inside the folded bias tape. Pin the tape in place. Be sure that the tape on the inside of the garment will be caught in the stitching when the tape is sewn from the right side. See pinning under Stitch in the Ditch on page 16, but instead of pinning in the ditch (because there is none), pin close to the edge of the tape on the outside of the garment, catching the tape on the inside of the garment.

Straight of the Grain Tape

Sometimes you will want to finish a seam in such a way that it has no give. To make straight of the grain tape, follow the directions above for bias tape, but cut the fabric following the grain arrows on the pattern pieces.

HEMS

As with most of the techniques in this book, hems can be made in a variety of ways. Stitching can show, stitching can be hidden (a blind hem), hems can be as narrow as possible, or they can be inches wide. Hems can even be left raw, allowing the edge to fray some. Lightweight fabrics tend toward narrow hems. Heavyweight fabrics tend to have single-fold hems. Hems used in the designs in this book include narrow, single-fold, double-fold, rolled, and raw.

Raw Edge

If you want a raw-edge hem, the process is very simple. Stitch two lines of topstitching approximately ½" to ¾" (13mm–2cm) from the bottom of the garment. The topstitching does not have to be a straight stitch; you can use a zigzag stitch or one of the decorative stitches on your machine. Remember that the purpose of these lines of stitching is to control how much the bottom edge frays.

Single-Fold Hem

Just as its name implies, a single-fold hem is folded once. The raw edge is finished by a serger, zigzagging, or seam binding, and the fabric is then folded up once to whatever length you want. The finished edge of the hem is then topstitched if you want the stitching to show; if you do not want the stitching to show, blind stitch by hand or follow the directions in your sewing machine manual for blind-hem stitching. Single-fold hems work best on heavier fabric and wider hems. If the garment has a curvy bottom, run a basting stitch along the raw edge and ease the curve in as you sew.

Double-Fold Hem

The double-fold hem is folded twice, thus eliminating a raw edge that needs to be finished. Often the double-fold hem is narrow, less than an inch (2.5cm) with both folds equal in size. Sometimes the first fold is narrower, about ½" (13mm), and the second fold is wider. Double-fold hems are almost always topstitched to the garment. These hems work best on lightweight fabrics when there isn't much curve to the hem.

If the skirt bottom is curved, use a narrow hem. The more curve, the narrower the hem should be, about 1/16" or 1/32" (1.5mm or 1mm). Practice making these narrow hems with a rolled-hem presser foot (see rolled hems, on the following page). Try it; you'll love it.

Rolled Hems

A rolled hem is usually used on sheer or very soft fabrics. A rolled hem is about as narrow as it is physically possible to make. Traditionally, this hem was made by rolling the edge between one's thumb and index finger and slip stitching with extraordinarily tiny stitches. Today, many sewing machines come with a special rolled-hem presser foot. If your machine did not come with this presser foot, they are available in sewing/craft supply catalogs.

WAISTBANDS

See the section on stitching in the ditch (page 16) for general directions on waistbands. Waistbands can be any width and are usually lined with fusible (or iron-on) interfacing. This helps the waistband keep its shape. Interfacing isn't really necessary for narrow bands. Waistbands are usually cut on the straight of the fabric. Before you cut, decide how you want the ends to come together. Do they butt up against each other? Is there an overlap or an underlap? Are you putting in a buttonhole? In any case, you have to finish the ends when the right sides are together. If there is an overlap or underlap, sew the extra length of the waistband edges together to the end of the waistband. Clip the corners and turn right side out.

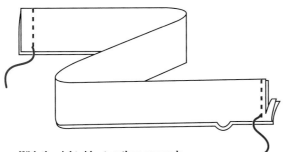

With the right sides together, sew ends of waistband together, trim, and turn.

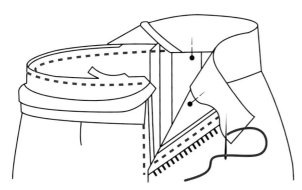

With the right side of the waistband to right side of garment, sew the waistband to the skirt.

BELTS, TIES, AND STRAPS

There are two basic methods for making tubes (such as belts, ties, and straps): stitch and turn, and fold and stitch.

Stitch and Turn

This method works best for really thin spaghetti straps and very lightweight fabric. With rights sides together, sew the long edges of the strip together using a ⅛" (3mm) seam allowance for narrow belts, ties, or straps and a ¼" (6mm) seam allowance for wider ones. Don't forget to sew one short end together. Clip the corners **(A)**. With a safety pin, chopstick, or turning tool, turn the tube right side out. Finish the open end by tucking in the seam allowance and stitching the end together. Don't trim the seam allowances before you turn the tube; the extra fabric gives body to the belt, tie, or strap **(B)**.

Fold and Stitch

This method is better for heavier fabrics. Follow the directions for making double-fold bias tape (page 19), except cut the fabric as directed for any given garment—some are on the bias, some are on the straight grain. Tuck in the seam allowances at both ends. With wrong sides together, topstitch the edges together. For extra body, topstitch the folded edge also.

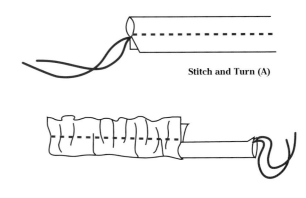

Stitch and Turn (A)

Stitch and Turn (B)

CASINGS

Several of the designs in this book have casings with elastic or ties. These casings are usually made by topstitching ¼" or ½" (6mm or 13mm) from the designated edge and inserting the tie or the appropriate length of elastic. Be sure to tack the elastic ends down by stitching in the seam allowance, preferably on top of another seam. Topstitch the tie in the middle of the back to keep the tie from escaping.

WELT POCKETS

Welt pockets are shown on the Annie Hall skirt (page 26), but they can be added to any garment for a more tailored appearance. These directions are for single welt pockets. You can also use a double welt or a single welt with a flap.

Prepare the Welt

Cut a piece of fabric the length of the pocket plus seam allowance, or use the welt pattern piece. Interface the welt if the fabric is not firm enough. Machine baste the interfacing to the fabric. Fold the welt in half with right sides facing. Stitch across both ends. Clip corners and turn right side out. Machine baste the raw edge.

Prepare the Fabric

With marking pencil, mark the placement of the pocket according to the pattern directions. Machine baste along the marked lines.

Attach the Welt and Pocket

With the raw edge of the welt touching the center cutting line, pin, and baste the right side of the welt to the right side of the garment. Pin and baste the pocket section in place over the welt **(A)**. From the wrong side, stitch on the basting lines on both sides of the center line. Do not stitch past the ends. Pull threads through to the wrong side and press. Carefully cut along the center line to approximately ¼" (6mm) from ends. Cut from center line diagonally to each of the four corners. Be careful not to clip the stitches. Turn the pocket pieces and welt to the inside **(B)**. Press all seam edges away from the opening. Pin the pocket sections together and stitch, being sure to catch the points at the top edges of the pocket **(C)**. On the right side, slip stitch the welt in place at each side.

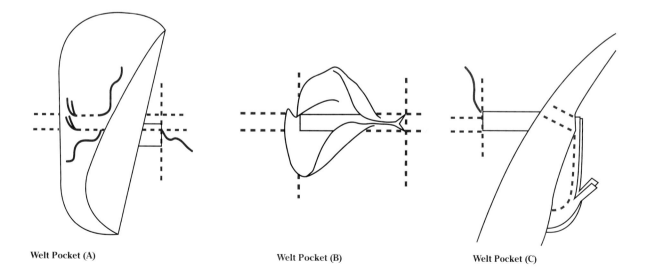

Welt Pocket (A)   **Welt Pocket (B)**   **Welt Pocket (C)**

EVERYDAY CHIC
SKIRTS

Skirts are one of the most versatile basics:
They range from slim pinstripe pencils to flirty, figure-friendly A-lines or
bias-cut evening numbers worthy of the red carpet. Skirts are the perfect base
from which to build your closet. The best news? They are fun to make and
easy to sew, and when you begin to understand how to mix fabrics
and style your look, the possibilities become infinite.

01

It's funny to think that skirt lengths were once seen as a sign of the times. Hemlines—rising or falling—were thought to indicate a bullish economy or an approaching recession until the sixties, when minis were linked to both increased prosperity and sexual adventurousness. These days they reflect little more than cyclic fashion trends, which is perfect for our purposes: When it comes to creating your own wardrobe from scratch, a skirt is the most straightforward garment to begin with.

In this chapter, I provide patterns for A-line, gored (fuller at the bottom), and straight skirts. The sewing projects you'll encounter here are organized from simplest to most complicated. Some add a yoke at the waistline, whereas others increase volume at the hem. I'll teach you how to introduce interesting details such as multipanels, pockets, pleats, and ruffles. When it comes to length, go ahead and experiment with a trendy mini, an office-appropriate knee length, or even a glamorous, floor-sweeping evening skirt.

Each sewing project comes with suggestions on how to do clever things with fabric. Just about any fabric can be used to make the skirt of your choice—wool or cotton blends, tweeds, silk charmeuse, chiffon and velvets are all Twinkle favorites—but the lining, which each of these skirts requires, should be in a fabric that has drape and movement.

The skirts in this chapter all have timeless silhouettes and the ability to move effortlessly from day to evening, weekday to weekend, or season to season. Simply experiment with fabrics or different styling—switch a cropped jacket for a cardigan, or trade a T-shirt for a camisole. These skirts are cut out in two main pieces, making them easy to fit and finish. Just think: You could be wearing your own custom skirt by this evening!

A PLUS
A-LINE

One skirt, two ways: Cerulean blue wool knitted tricot gives structure to this perfect winter workweek skirt, but if you want to create a look that's more luxe, make it in shiny fabric such as brocade, duchesse satin, or gold Lurex™. A ladylike chiffon blouse will float above the heavier fabric of your A-line. For a whimsical take, try this pattern in embroidered silk.

TWINKLE TIP
Add contrasting piping between the yoke and skirt to take the detail up a stylish notch.

Instructions on page 40.

ANNIE HALL

This full-length wool, nylon, and Lycra™ tweed skirt isn't your traditional long, straight skirt. This one is cut on the bias, which helps it to fit snugly but still allows for easy walking and sitting. The bias cut also gives it a mermaid shape. Fishtail shapes are usually made with a flowing fabric like silk charmeuse, but we've turned that idea on its head by using tweed and leaving the edges unfinished. (Because the fabric is cut on the bias, the raw edges won't fray.)

Add welt pockets to the front of your skirt for a touch of seventies style, and don't be afraid to top it off with a mix of stripes and prints. For a tongue-in-cheek take, try a bohemian "evening look" by topping the skirt with a silk blouse and finishing the look with metallic flats and smoky makeup, perfect for a gallery opening or a night on the town.

TWINKLE TIP
Fabric cut on the bias will stretch out, so hang the skirt for two days before finishing your hem.

Instructions on page 43.

SKYLINE SKIRT

Houndstooth is a classic motif that will keep coming back into style, so why not play with panels, color, and pattern? Choose compatible fabric with a similar weight—we've used cotton gabardine and wool houndstooth—and experiment with an edgy jagged line between the yoke and the eight-panel skirt that echoes the houndstooth pattern. Try solid two-tone colors: brown on top and bright tangerine on the bottom, or, for a graphic look, black on top and cream on the bottom. For something cleaner and more sophisticated, choose two different fabrics in the exact same color, such as black wool on top and black brocade with Lurex on the bottom, or cream tweed on top and heavyweight cream charmeuse on the bottom. Colored tights and an oversize knit scarf amp up the look for day.

TWINKLE TIP
Small adjustments in seam direction can dramatically change the look of this skirt. Instead of the jagged line, try to make the seams slant across the whole skirt in a horizontal direction to achieve a clean and crisp look. For an homage to brights, cut out the skirt into more than eight panels and choose a different color for each.

Instructions on page 46.

MASC
ET

ULIN FEMININ

This pinstriped straight skirt in a wool-and-Lycra blend brilliantly brings sex appeal and glamour to an office staple. Perennial pinstripes are no longer stuffy when powder-pink satin, scalloped-edge lace, and ribbon are added to the mix. Layer the lace over the satin and then finish with a chic ribbon waistband. A cardigan in a fresh lemon hue is a pretty alternative to a jacket.

TWINKLE TIP
Play with the idea of layering lace over fabric. For a sexy cocktail skirt, make a simple pencil skirt in lavender silk charmeuse, then overlay black lace to cover the entire skirt, leaving about 1" to 2" (2.5cm–5cm) untrimmed at the hem.

Instructions on page 48.

LITTLE BLACK SKIRT

This truncated silhouette is as versatile as a little black dress—youthful without being too trendy. Making the skirt from one of the many novelty fabrics on the market gives you even more pizzazz. I chose a black brocade of wool blended with polyamide and viscose and woven with a shiny Lurex thread that gives the fabric an extra sparkle. The hemline pleats are cut on the bias and the edges are left raw to pep up this classic preppy miniskirt. Use a matte fabric for the pleats in the same color as the Lurex but a different texture to give it a clean, modern finish. Let the Lurex shine through by pairing it with a light-colored tunic on top.

TWINKLE TIP
To turn this skirt into a classic Chanel-inspired number, make it in pastel wool bouclé. Remove the pleats and elongate the skirt by 1" to 2" (2.5cm–5cm). Add belt loops and finish it off with a gold chain belt.

Instructions on page 51.

ENGLISH
GARDEN

Made of brown and tangerine vintage-print silk charmeuse with a shirred brown chiffon yoke, this flippy skirt is fun to wear. It is a challenging shape to sew, thanks to the multiple panels and godets (the triangular pieces inserted between panels). But don't be put off: Each panel is a repeat of the one before, so it's easier than it looks. There are eight panels in all, and the size of the flare depends on the size of the triangle used for the godet piece. This skirt has a front opening with twelve or thirteen covered buttons with fabric loops. Take this floral skirt out of the garden and make it pop by pairing it with a bright argyle sweater.

TWINKLE TIP
For a quieter, more versatile skirt, make the yoke and the skirt in a solid neutral color such as gray, taupe, or navy, and wear it with a sweater or jacket for day or a sexy camisole at night.

Instructions on page 54.

JAZZ HALL

This skirt is made of thick wool knitted tricot with a four-flounce bottom edge. I chose poppy red with a contrasting butter yellow. Fabric chosen for drape and body is cut on the bias and forms a natural ruffle (make that a double). When shopping for fabric, gather your choices in your hand to make sure they will shape easily into folds. Because the fabric I chose is tightly structured and the flounces are cut on the bias, the unfinished edges do not fray. The raw-edge "finish" gives this seemingly preppy knee-length skirt an edgier look. Finish with a natty narrow waistband. For a quirky, completely different look, try a large houndstooth fabric with just one layer of ruffles.

TWINKLE TIP
To adjust any of these skirt patterns to best fit your body, find a sewing buddy. You'll need two to three yards (1.8m–2.7m) of muslin or any leftover fabric that has a steady structure, the shoes you would wear with the skirt, and about an hour to get it right (your buddy is the one pinning the muslin around you). But once you're done, this base pattern can be used to create a whole closet of different skirt styles.

Instructions on page 58.

INSTRUCTIONS

& technical notes

1.

2.

3.

While the number of different designs for skirts is almost infinite, there are a few basics that will help you create a skirt that fits perfectly and also frees you to add your own personality to the design. There are a few "lines" in a skirt design to keep in mind. There are three horizontal lines: the waist line, the hip line, and the bottom line (the hem). There are two to four other lines, or at least points of interest, and those are the vertical lines: two side seams, and the optional front and

back center seams. Occasionally, as in gored skirts, there can be many more vertical seams. I have included two gored skirt designs, each with eight seams (English Garden and Skyline Skirt); two A-line skirts (Jazz Hall and A Plus A-Line); and three straight skirts (Annie Hall, Masculin et Feminin, and the Little Black Skirt).

All of the skirts have invisible zippers in the left side seam, except for the English Garden, which has covered buttons

and fabric loops in the front center seam. All of the skirts are lined, except, again, the English Garden, in which only the yoke is lined. If you choose not to include a lining and the skirt does not have a waistband, you will have to figure out how to finish the waist edge. The only skirt that really needs a lining is the Jazz Hall, because two of its flounces are attached to the lining.

Since everyone's body is different and everyone's taste about ease and look

4.

5.

6.

7.

is different, I recommend basting the skirt pieces together without the zipper, trying on the skirt, and adjusting the seams or darts (or both) to fit your body. Note: On the English Garden and the Skyline Skirt, it is very important to baste the seams together and try the skirt on. Because there are so many seams—eight—changing the seam allowance only slightly can change the size of the skirt significantly.) As for length, in today's fashion climate, skirts can be any length you want. I've suggested lengths for these skirts, but don't be afraid to lengthen or shorten them according to your taste.

Four of the skirts have yokes: English Garden, A Plus A-Line, Masculin et Feminin, and Little Black Skirt. On many skirts with yokes, the yoke goes from the waist line to the hip line, but you can vary the width of the yoke to suit your taste. On the Little Black Skirt, for example, I have designed a very narrow yoke. The Annie Hall skirt looks like it has a waistband, but it actually functions as a very narrow yoke.

The steps for putting these skirts together are more or less the same, but each skirt has its own unique design and embellishments. Feel free to change the order of steps to whatever makes the most sense to you. Remember, there are many ways of doing the same thing. Go with what you know and are comfortable with; I only offer suggestions as to the order of the steps.

A PLUS A-LINE PAGE 24

For this skirt, sew two seams, make four pleats, sew the yoke to the skirt, hem it, and you are good to go. If using lighter-weight fabric, revise the pleats by adding more folds, but ensure that each fold is shallower. To create a more controlled hip contour and flowing hemline, stitch down the pleats for 1" to 2" (2.5cm–5cm).

SKILL LEVEL   EASY

MATERIALS

1¾ yd (1.6m) wool tricot

1¾ yd (1.6m) lightweight lining fabric

⅜ yd (34cm) fusible interfacing

Thread*

7"–9" (18cm–23cm) invisible zipper

1 hook and eye

seam allowances

½" (13mm) for the yoke, side seams, and skirt waistband;

¾" (2cm) skirt hem; 1" (2.5cm) lining hem; ⅜" (9.5mm) for all other seams

* This skirt has three lines of stitching that show on the right side of the garment: ¼" (6mm) below the waistline, ⅜" (9.5mm) above the yoke-skirt seam, and approximately 1" (2.5cm) above the hem. Plan your thread color to match or contrast.

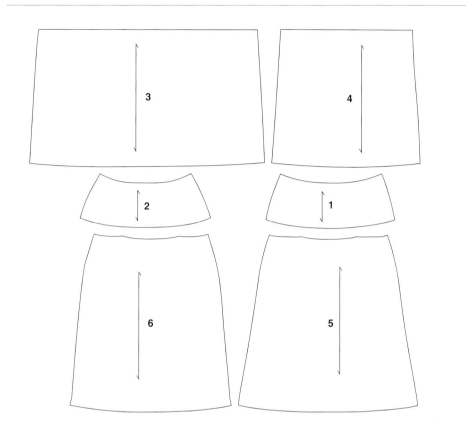

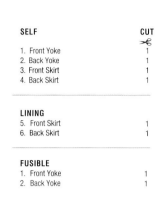

SELF	CUT
1. Front Yoke	1
2. Back Yoke	1
3. Front Skirt	1
4. Back Skirt	1

LINING	
5. Front Skirt	1
6. Back Skirt	1

FUSIBLE	
1. Front Yoke	1
2. Back Yoke	1

1 Select the pattern size according to your hip measurement plus 2"–4" (5cm–10cm) ease. Lay out the pattern pieces on the corresponding fabrics, fitting them on the fabric however works for you, and cut. Don't forget to watch the grain lines.

2 Baste together the right-hand side seam of the front yoke (1) and back yoke (2). Try on the yoke and pin together the zipper edge. Make the yoke fit comfortably on your waist and hips by adjusting the seam allowances. Mark the new seam allowances. Remove the basting. Trim the seam allowances off the fusible interfacing to match the finished size (after seaming) of each of the yoke pieces (1, 2). Press the fusible interfacing to the wrong side of the corresponding yoke piece.

3 Starting with the skirt front (3), pin the pleats following the arrows: Pin point 1 to point 2 and point 3 to point 4 on both sides of the center. Baste the pleats in place by hand.

4 With right sides together and aligning the center fronts and side seams, pin the front yoke (1) to the skirt front (3). Note: If you have made any changes to the size of the yoke, you will have to adjust the pleats accordingly. When you are satisfied that everything matches up, place the right sides of the front yoke and skirt front together, with the bottom edge of the yoke flush with the top of the skirt, and sew the front yoke to the skirt front. To reduce some of the bulk at the seam line, grade the inner seam allowances, leaving the outer seam allowance at ½" (13mm). Press all seam allowances up toward the yoke. On the inside of the skirt, open the ½" (13mm) seam allowance so it lays against the yoke, then sew the seam allowance to the yoke about ⅜" (9.5mm) from the existing seam line. The bobbin stitches will show on the right side of the skirt, so be sure to have the thread color you want in the bobbin. **(A)**

5 Repeat step 4 with the back yoke (2) and skirt back (4). Before sewing the side seams with right sides together,

A

put the zipper in the left side seam following the directions on the package or using your favorite method; finish sewing the left side seam. Then sew the right side seam. Be sure the front and back yoke lines meet at the side seams.

6 Finish the hem according to your favorite method. I have sewn a single-fold hem with the stitches showing on the outside of the skirt for a sporty look. Note: If using fabric that frays easily, don't forget to finish the bottom edge of the hem before turning.

7 Adjust the darts on the front and back lining pieces (5, 6) to fit the skirt. With the right sides of the front and back lining pieces together, sew the side seams of the lining together, leaving a 7"–9" (18cm–23cm) opening on the left-hand side seam and an 8" (20.5cm) opening at the hem edge of the left side seam. Finish the 8" (20.5cm) slit with a ¼" (6mm) double-fold hem.

8 If you are sure the lining is not going to show below the skirt at the hemline, hem the lining with a ¼" (6mm) double-fold hem. If you are unsure, leave the lining hem until last.

9 Pin the lining to the skirt with right sides together, aligning the side seams and the zipper opening. Using a ½" (13mm) seam allowance, sew the lining to the skirt around the waist edge. You may want to grade the seam to eliminate some bulk; understitching is also an option. Turn the lining to the inside. Press the top edge so that the lining doesn't show above the waist line. Slip stitch the lining opening to the zipper tape. Topstitch the waist edge ¼" (6mm) from the top.

10 Adjust the lining hem. If you haven't already, finish the lining with a ¼" (6mm) double-fold hem.

Finishing Touches

11 With sewing thread, crochet a chain about 2" (5cm) long. Attach one end at the bottom of the lining on the right-hand seam line. Attach the other end to the seam allowance of the skirt. This will help to keep the lining from sliding around.

12 Sew a hook and eye on the inside the of waist edge above the zipper.

ANNIE HALL

PAGE 26

The Annie Hall is easier to make than it looks: Seam all skirt pieces together, and then join the waistband and the lining. To avoid bulkiness at the waist, don't fold the tweed in half. Instead, use the lining to make your facing. Alternatively, to create an old Hollywood glamour look, piece together the four bottom pieces but keep the center front and center back seam, get rid of the pockets, roll hem it in, and make it in heavyweight silk satin in a sophisticated color. Skip the welt pockets in step 3 and the skill level changes to easy.

SKILL LEVEL   INTERMEDIATE

MATERIALS

2 yd (1.8m) wool, nylon, and Lycra–blend tweed

2 yd (1.8m) lightweight lining fabric

¹/₂ yd (45.5cm) fusible interfacing

Matching thread

7"–9" (18cm–23cm) invisible zipper

seam allowances

¹/₂" (13mm) throughout, unless otherwise indicated

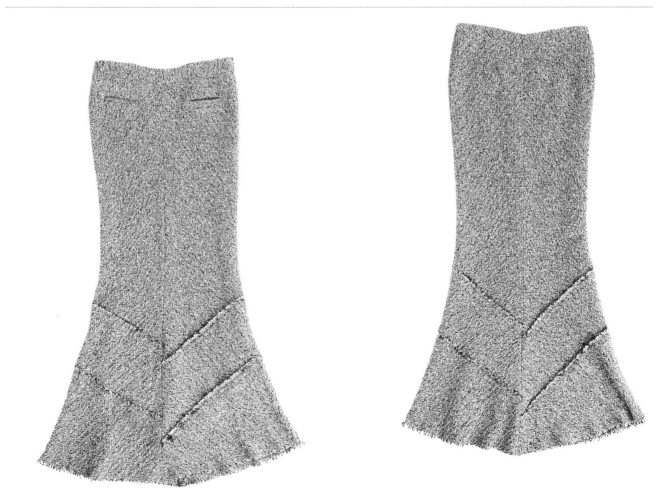

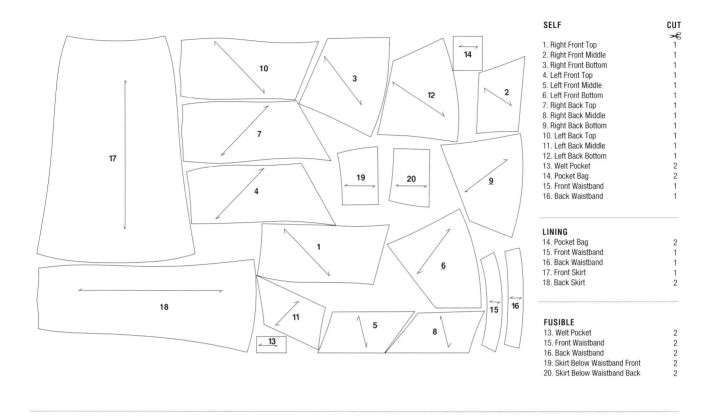

SELF	CUT
1. Right Front Top	1
2. Right Front Middle	1
3. Right Front Bottom	1
4. Left Front Top	1
5. Left Front Middle	1
6. Left Front Bottom	1
7. Right Back Top	1
8. Right Back Middle	1
9. Right Back Bottom	1
10. Left Back Top	1
11. Left Back Middle	1
12. Left Back Bottom	1
13. Welt Pocket	2
14. Pocket Bag	2
15. Front Waistband	1
16. Back Waistband	1

LINING	
14. Pocket Bag	2
15. Front Waistband	1
16. Back Waistband	1
17. Front Skirt	1
18. Back Skirt	2

FUSIBLE	
13. Welt Pocket	2
15. Front Waistband	2
16. Back Waistband	2
19. Skirt Below Waistband Front	2
20. Skirt Below Waistband Back	2

1 Select the pattern size according to your hip or waist measurement, whichever is larger. You do not have to allow for ease because of the stretch of the fabric. The bias cut makes it easy to stretch the pieces out of shape, so take extra care when cutting and sewing. (When sewing, try not to pull the edges.) Lay out the pattern pieces on the corresponding fabrics, fitting them on the fabric however works for you, and cut. Don't forget to watch the grain lines.

2 Press the fusible interfacing pieces (19, 20) to the top edge of the front top (1, 4) and back top (7, 10); fuse interfacing to the waistband (15, 16) and waistband lining (15, 16).

3 To add pockets, follow the directions for Welt Pockets (page 21). Insert pockets into the front top pieces (1, 4) where indicated.

4 Sew darts on the back top pieces (7, 10). Lay out the pieces in order according to the diagram. **(A)** With two lines of topstitching, sew the right side of piece 2 to the wrong side of piece 3, leaving the upper raw edge of piece 3 showing and pointing up. Repeat with pieces 5 to 6, 8 to 9, and 11 to 12. Then sew pieces 1 to 2, 4 to 5, 7 to 8, and 10 to 11 in the same way.

5 Using ½" (13mm) seam allowances and with right sides together, sew the center front and center back seams, matching all points.

6 With rights sides together, sew the front waistband (15) to the skirt front and the back waistband (16) to the skirt back. Note: This waistband is put on more like a narrow yoke rather than the traditional waistband.

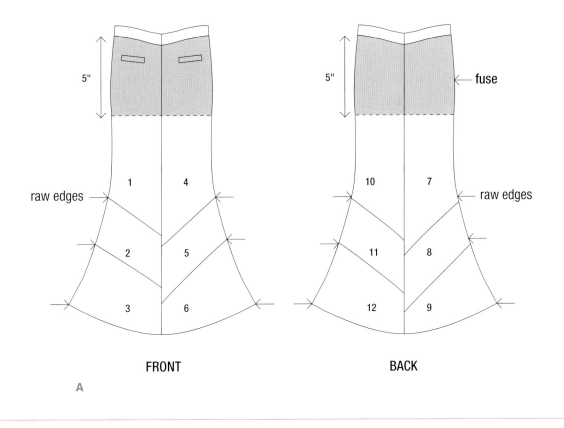

FRONT

BACK

5"

5"

fuse

raw edges

raw edges

1   4

10   7

2   5

11   8

3   6

12   9

A

7 Using your favorite method or following the directions on the package, insert the zipper in the left side seam with the top of the zipper at the top of the waistband. Finish sewing the left side seam, then sew the right-hand side seam together.

8 Adjust the pleats where indicated on the back skirt lining (18) to fit the back waistband (16). Sew the front waistband lining (15) to the front lining (17). With ½" (13mm) seam allowances and rights sides together, sew the side seams together, leaving a 7"–9" (18cm–23cm) opening for the zipper in the left-hand seam. With right sides together, sew the lining to the skirt at the waist. Clip and grade the seam allowance. Understitch.

Finishing Touches

9 Turn the skirt to the right side. Slip stitch the lining to the zipper tape. Before finishing, hang the skirt for a few days to allow the fabric to stretch out. Cut the bottom of the hem line even (this skirt has a raw hem) and sew two lines of stitching: Make the first one ½" (13mm) from the bottom and the second about ½" (13mm) above the first. This will allow for controlled fraying. Trim the lining so that it does not show below the skirt hem. Hem the lining with a ½" (13mm) double-fold hem.

10 With thread, crochet a chain about 2" (5cm) long. Attach one end at the bottom hem of the lining on the right-hand seam allowance. Attach the other end to the seam allowance of the skirt. This will help to keep the lining from sliding around.

SKYLINE SKIRT

PAGE 28

This eight-gore A-line skirt has a solid top and houndstooth bottom in an interesting geometric design. The two front and two back panels mirror each other; the same goes for the side panels. Join each top panel to a bottom panel, and then each panel to the next. Finish your side seams and join the lining at the waist. To make this skirt fit, you will have to do some measuring and very accurate cutting and sewing. The reality is that if you miscalculate cutting or sewing by even ⅛" (3mm) on both sides of each panel, the waistline, for example, could be 2" (5cm) too big or too small.

SKILL LEVEL   INTERMEDIATE

MATERIALS

1 yd (1m) patterned wool houndstooth (self)

1 yd (1m) solid-colored cotton gabardine (combo)

1 yd (1m) lightweight lining fabric

Matching thread

7"–9" (18cm–23cm) invisible zipper

1 hook and eye

seam allowances

½" (13mm) for the side seams; 1½" (3.8cm) hem; ⅜" (9.5mm) for all other seams

1   Select the pattern size according to your hip measurement plus 2"–4" (5cm–10cm) ease. Divide your actual waist and hip measurements each by 8. To these numbers, add 1" (2.5cm) for seam allowances. Measure pattern pieces (1, 2) at the waist and hip lines. These measurements should be equal to the ones you calculated for your measurements. For example, the width of the pattern piece at the waist should equal your waist divided by 8 plus 1. Adjust the pattern pieces to fit. Remember, it is better to make the skirt slightly larger rather than smaller; if necessary, it is much easier to make the skirt smaller after you have sewn all the seams.

2   Lay out the pattern pieces, but before you cut out the pieces, mark the tops, bottoms, and sides of each piece in the seam allowance to indicate the placement of each piece. This will help you find their corresponding pieces, since they all look very similar. While cutting, lay the pieces in order on a table or on the floor. There are 16 pieces to put together, and it is very easy to get mixed up.

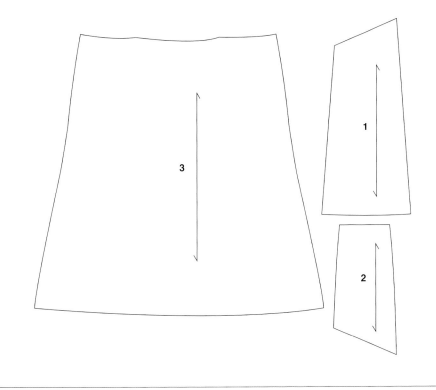

SELF	CUT ✂
1. Front and Back Bottom	8
COMBO	
2. Front and Back Yoke	8
LINING	
3. Front and Back	2

3 Using ½" (13mm) seam allowances, sew each yoke piece (2) to its corresponding bottom piece (1). After sewing the pieces together, keep them in order on the table or floor. Sew the front pieces together at the side edges and then sew the back pieces together at the side edges; leave the skirt's right and left side seams between the front and the back unstitched. Note: If you are concerned about the fit, baste the seams together. Pin the right-hand seam together and try the skirt on. If you have to adjust the size, try to evenly distribute the change across all of the seams, and sew the seams accordingly. Remember, the right and left seams should be at your sides. If you make all of the adjustment in just one seam, you may inadvertently shift the side seams too much.

4 Put a zipper into the left side seam using your favorite method or the directions on the package. Finish sewing the left seam below the zipper and then sew the right-hand side seam.

5 Finish the bottom edge with your favorite hem. I made a 1½" (3.8cm) single-fold blind-stitched hem.

6 If you have altered any seam allowance on the skirt, make the same amount of change in the darts at the waistline of the lining. Sew the darts in the front and back lining pieces (3) as indicated. Sew the side seams together, leaving an opening for the zipper in the left-hand seam. Finish the lining with a ¾" (2cm) double-fold hem. With the right sides together and aligning the side seams, sew the waist edge of the lining to the waist edge of the skirt with a ½" (13mm) seam allowance. Clip and grade the seam. Understitching is optional. Turn the lining to the inside.

Finishing Touches

7 Slip stitch the lining to the zipper opening. Sew a line of topstitching around the waist, ¼" (6mm) from the edge.

8 Sew a hook and eye to the waist at the top of the zipper.

MASCULIN ET FEMININ PAGE 30

This striking black and champagne-pink straight skirt sports a silk-satin yoke overlaid with a black scalloped-edge lace. The pattern takes the basic skirt pattern and adds a seam across the hips. An inverted kick pleat is sewn into the back to offer ease of movement. A black silk tie waistband tops off the look.

SKILL LEVEL   EASY

MATERIALS

³/₄ yd (70cm) pinstriped wool-and-Lycra blend for skirt (self)

³/₈ yd (34cm) black silk satin or charmeuse for waistband and tie (combo 1)

³/₈ yd (34cm) silk satin for yoke (combo 2)

³/₈ yd (34cm) lightweight lace* (combo 3)

1 yd (1m) lining or lightweight acetate fabric

³/₈ yd (34cm) very lightweight fusible interfacing

Matching thread

7"–9" (18cm–23cm) invisible zipper

1 hook and eye

seam allowances

¹/₂" (13mm) for the side seams; ³/₈" (9.5mm) for all other seams

* You may be able to find 6" (15cm) lace in the trimming section of the fabric store. This lace is sold by the yard or meter. Purchase enough to go around your hips plus a few extra inches or centimeters. You can also purchase lace that's wider than desired and trim the edge according to the lace design. You might end up with lace that does not have a scalloped edge but instead a zigzag or other interesting shape.

1   Select the pattern size according to your hip measurement plus 2"–5" (5cm–10cm) ease. Lay out the pattern pieces on the corresponding fabrics, fitting them on the fabric however works for you, and cut. Don't forget to watch the grain lines.

2   Baste the front yoke (5) and back yoke (6) pieces together at the right-hand side seam. Try it on and pin the left side seam together. Adjust the fit on your waist and hips by adjusting the seam allowances and back darts. Mark any

changes and adjust the lining and the skirt bottom to match.

3   On the skirt back pieces (2), press the fusible interfacing (9) to the wrong side of the back slit opening.

4   Aligning the top and side edges, baste the wrong side of the back lace yoke (8) to the right side of the back yoke (6). Baste the wrong side of the front lace yoke (7) to the right side of the front yoke (5), aligning the top and side

edges in the same way. Treating the lace and silk as one piece by lining them up at center front and center back, make the darts where indicated.

5 With right sides together and using a ½" (13mm) seam allowance, stitch together the skirt back pieces (2) at the back center seam, stopping at the top of the kick pleat opening. Sew the back yoke (6) to the skirt back (2) and the front yoke (5) to the skirt front (1). Be careful not to catch the lace in the seam. Note: Be sure to match the seams on the front and back where the yoke meets the skirt. Put a zipper into the left side seam using your favorite method or following the directions on the package. Finish sewing the left side seam.

6 On the right-hand side seam of the front and back yoke pieces, remove about 2" (5cm) of the basting stitches holding the lace to the yoke. Sewing on just the lace, sew the

side seam of the lace overlay together with right sides facing. Note: You may want to sew this seam as a French seam to hide the raw edges. In this case, with a scant ¼" (6mm) seam allowance, sew the seam first with wrong sides together, then resew the seam with the right sides together, enclosing the previous seam allowance within this seam. Then, with right sides together, sew the right side seam of the skirt together, being careful to match the front and back yoke seams and avoiding the lace. Baste the lace to the yoke at the waist.

7 Sew the front skirt lining (10) and back skirt lining (11, 12) together at the side seams, leaving a 7"–9" (18cm–23cm) opening for the zipper on the left side seam. Adjust and baste the pleats on the back lining to fit the skirt back. Make a ½" (13mm) double-fold hem on the bottom of the lining.

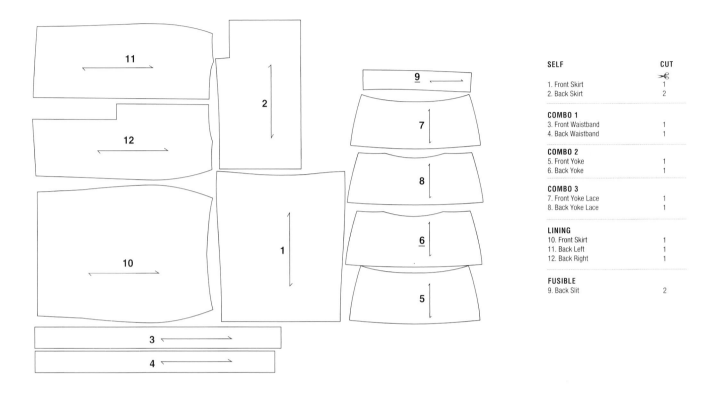

SELF	CUT ✂
1. Front Skirt	1
2. Back Skirt	2
COMBO 1	
3. Front Waistband	1
4. Back Waistband	1
COMBO 2	
5. Front Yoke	1
6. Back Yoke	1
COMBO 3	
7. Front Yoke Lace	1
8. Back Yoke Lace	1
LINING	
10. Front Skirt	1
11. Back Left	1
12. Back Right	1
FUSIBLE	
9. Back Slit	2

8 On the center line of the back lining piece, stay stitch a V of reinforcing stitches the length of the kick pleat as indicated on the pattern piece. Sew a second line of stay stitches on top of the first line for about 2" (5cm) on each side of the point of the V.

9 Carefully cut a slit in the lining to the point of the V.

10 With right sides together, pin the lining to the skirt at the waist edge, matching the side seams and zipper opening.

11 Make the kick pleat: With right sides still together, hand-baste the back seam line of the lining to the back seam line of the skirt. This will help you sew the next part without getting a bubble in either the lining or the skirt. With a ¼" (6mm) seam allowance and sewing from top to bottom, sew the lining slit edge to the kick pleat edge.

12 Press the folds. Sew a line of stitching very close to the edge on the inside kick pleat piece.

13 Stitch across the top of the pleat to hold it in place.

14 Remove the basting stitches from the back seam and turn the lining to the inside. Baste the top of the skirt to the lining. Slip stitch the lining to the zipper tape.

Finishing Touches

15 With right sides together, sew a short end of the waistband strips (3, 4) together to make one long strip.

16 Attach the strip to the skirt like a waistband using the stitch in the ditch method (page16). The ties of the strip were sewn with the stitch and turn method (page 20); use either this or the fold and stitch method (page 20)—it doesn't matter which. Just remember to match the right-hand side seam of the skirt with the seam of the waistband strip.

17 Sew a hook and eye on the inside top edge of the skirt above the zipper.

LITTLE BLACK SKIRT

This sexy, short black skirt is quick to sew and fun to wear. It has a 2" (5cm) yoke, a pleated hem line, and it is embellished with pockets and black double-fold bias tape, which you can purchase or make yourself (page 19). There is no waistband, but it does have a mini yoke that looks like a waistband.

SKILL LEVEL EASY

MATERIALS

³/₄ yd (70cm) synthetic-blend fabric* (self)

¹/₂ yd (45.5cm) black fabric for yoke lining, hem and waistband binding, and optional pocket trim (combo)

¹/₂ yd (45.5cm) lightweight lining fabric

¹/₂ yd (45.5cm) fusible interfacing

Matching thread

7"–9" (18cm–23cm) invisible zipper

1 hook and eye

seam allowances

¹/₂" (13mm) for the side seams;
³/₈" (9.5mm) for all other seams

* A synthetic blend will help stabilize the pleats. I chose a wool-and-Lurex brocade blended with polyamide and viscose.

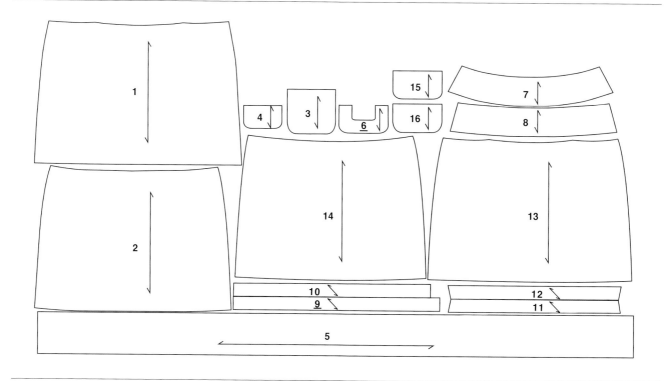

1 Select the pattern size according to your hip measure-ment plus 2"–4" (5cm–10cm) ease. Lay out the pattern pieces on the corresponding fabrics, fitting them on the fabric however works for you, and cut. Don't forget to watch the grain lines.

2 Baste the yoke facing (7, 8) to the corresponding skirt front and back linings (13, 14). Baste together at the right-hand side seam. Try it on and pin the zipper edge together. Adjust the seam allowances at the waist and hip line to fit comfortably. Don't forget to make the same changes on the skirt pieces.

3 Press fusible interfacing on pieces (3, 4, 5, 7, 8) where indicated.

4 I have embellished this miniskirt with two patch pockets and flaps, but they are optional. If you want to trim the pocket flaps, do that first by sewing the binding (6) to the pocket flap (4). Clip and grade the seam, turn, and press the pocket flap. **(A)**

5 Line the pocket flaps by sewing the right side of the flap lining (15) to the right side of the flap (4) with a ¼" (6mm) seam allowance, leaving the top edge open. Trim the seams, clip the corners, and turn the pocket flap right side out. Press flat. Serge or zigzag the top edges together.

6 With right sides together, pin the pocket lining (16) to the top of the pocket (3). Fold down the pocket ½" (13mm) from the top, right side facing in, matching the bottom edges of the pocket and the pocket lining. Sew 3 sides of the pocket together, but *not the top*; leave a small opening in the bottom for turning.

7 Trim the seams and clip the corners. Turn the pocket right side out. Press flat. Slip stitch the opening closed. Place and pin the pockets on the skirt front (1) about 1½" (3.8cm) from the side seam line and about 2" (5cm) below the yoke line. Topstitch the pocket in place.

8 Lay the right side of the pocket flap (4) on the right side of the skirt ½" (13mm) from the top of the pocket. (The in-side, untrimmed edge of the flap should be close to the pocket top, and the curved edge is facing the front yoke.) Line up both side edges.

9 Sew the flaps to the skirt front using a ¼" (6mm) seam allowance. Press the flap down toward the pocket and topstitch the top edge of the flap.

10 Sew the darts in the skirt back (2). Sew the front yoke (7) to the skirt front (1) and the back yoke (8) to the skirt back (2). Press the seams toward the yoke. Topstitch the binding

SELF	CUT ✂
1. Front	1
2. Back	1
3. Patch Pocket	2
4. Pocket Flap	2
5. Hem Pleats	2
7. Front Yoke	1
8. Back Yoke	1

COMBO	
6. Pocket Binding	2
7. Front Yoke	1
8. Back Yoke	1
9. Front Hem Binding	1
10. Back Hem Binding	1
11. Front Waistband Binding	1
12. Back Waistband Binding	1

LINING	
13. Front Skirt	1
14. Back Skirt	1
15. Pocket Flap	2
16. Patch Pocket	2

FUSIBLE	
3. Patch Pocket	2
4. Pocket Flap	2
5. Hem Pleats	2
7. Front Yoke	2
8. Back Yoke	2

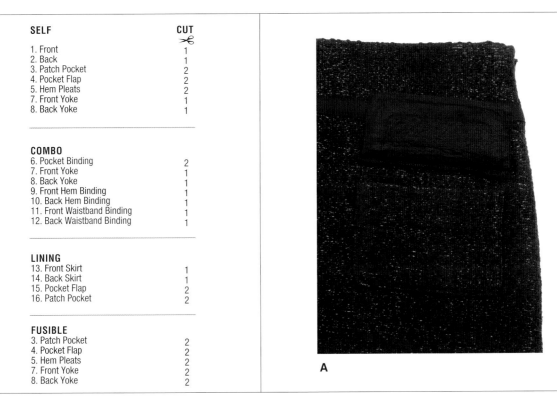

A

over the front and back yoke seam line, with the bottom of the tape sitting in the seam line.

11 Before sewing the side seams together, put the zipper in the left side seam, using your favorite method or following the package directions, then finish sewing the left seam. Sew the right-hand side seam. Be sure the front and back yoke lines meet at the sides.

12 With right sides together, sew the hem pleat bands (5) together at both ends, making a circle. Fold the hem pleat band in half lengthwise with wrong sides together. Baste the open edge together ¼" (6mm) from the edge. I used 1" (2.5cm) pleats, but how wide you make the pleats is up to you; if you want to get fancy, make the pleat widths different. Adjusting the number and width of the pleats to the bottom of your skirt takes a little fiddling (I had 36 pleats); try to hide the band's side seams inside the pleats. Pin the pleats in place on the band. Pin the pleated band to the skirt bottom, with the right side of the pleat to the wrong side of skirt, aligning the side seams and the bottom edge of the skirt with the top edge of the band. Don't worry! The seam allowance is supposed to end up on the right side of the skirt. We'll fix that next. Make any final adjustments to the pleats. With a ¼" (6mm) seam allowance, sew the hem pleats to the skirt. Press the seam up toward the skirt.

13 On the right side of the skirt, topstitch the binding over the seam allowance, setting the bottom edge of the tape in the seam line.

14 Sew the front yoke (7) to the front skirt lining (13) and the back yoke (8) to the back skirt lining (14). Sew the side seams together, leaving an opening the length of your zipper on the left-hand side. Pin the lining to the skirt, with right sides together, aligning the side seams and zipper opening. Using a ½" (13mm) seam allowance, sew the lining to the skirt around the waist edge. Clip, trim, and understitch the seam. Turn the lining to the inside. Slip stitch the lining to the zipper tape. Finish the lining with a ½" (13mm) double-fold hem.

Finishing Touches

15 On the inside right-hand side seam between the lining and the skirt, tack the lining yoke seam allowance to the skirt yoke seam allowance. This will help to keep the lining from sliding around.

16 Sew a hook and eye on the inside top edge of the skirt above the zipper.

ENGLISH GARDEN

This skirt is constructed by inserting triangular godets into the eight gore seams. To make this skirt fit, you will have to do some measuring and very accurate cutting and sewing. Sew each panel to a godet piece and then join the panels. Once you've joined the front and back pieces, shirring on the yoke will create a romantic line. Start with a larger piece of fabric and then shirr it into the yoke. Savvy sewers stitch the shirring on the princess line (page 17) to stabilize it. Add the front and back yokes and then sew the side seams. For button loops, mark the placement of each one and then sandwich it between the yoke and the facing. If you'd like to skip the button closure, add a side zipper instead, but keep the buttons in front as a decorative detail. To add glamour, use jewel-tone glass buttons.

SKILL LEVEL INTERMEDIATE

MATERIALS

1 yd (1m) silk charmeuse, satin, or challis (self)

1/2 yd (45.5cm) coordinating chiffon for yoke (combo)

1/2 yd (45.5cm) lining fabric for yoke

1/2 yd (45.5cm) fusible interfacing

Matching thread

Button loop tape (if you do not want to make fabric loops)

1/3 yd (30.5cm) of 1/4" (6mm) single-fold bias tape

Twelve 1/2" (13mm) buttons*

seam allowances

1/2" (13mm) throughout unless otherwise indicated

* I made covered buttons from the yoke fabric, but any small buttons will work. The buttons are lined up, almost touching each other. The exact number of buttons depends on the size of the button and the length of the yoke.

1 Select the pattern size according to your hip or waist measurement plus 2"–4" (5cm–10cm), whichever is larger. Lay out and cut the pattern pieces for the back yoke lining (5) and the left and right front yoke lining pieces (8).

2 Baste the left and right front yoke lining pieces (8) to the back yoke lining (5) at the side seams. Try on the lining and pin the front seam together. Adjust the fit on your waist and hips by adjusting the seam allowances. If you have to adjust the lining by more than 1½" (3.8cm), try a different size.

3 After you have adjusted the yoke lining to fit your body, measure the bottom edge of the yoke lining and divide this number by 8, and add 1" (2.5cm). Measure the top edge of the skirt flare piece (1). This measurement should be equal to the one you calculated for the bottom edge of the yoke. If not, adjust the pattern piece accordingly. Remember, it is better to make the skirt slightly larger rather than smaller. Because this is a flippy skirt, it is OK to have more ease at the hipline than you usually have.

4   Lay out and cut the remaining pattern pieces on the corresponding fabrics, fitting them on the fabric however works for you, and cut. Mark the left and right side of each piece in the seam allowance.

5   Lay out the fabric pieces on the table or floor in order. Pin 1 godet (2) to each skirt flare (1). Be sure to pin them all along the same side edge. It doesn't matter which side you pick, just do them all the same. **(B)**

6   Sew 1 godet (2) to 1 skirt flare (1). Replace each piece on the table or floor in the same order. Repeat with the remaining 7 godets and skirt flares. Sew the gores together. There should be 1 triangle at the bottom of the skirt flares between each gore seam. Leave the top of the center front seam open approximately 2½" (6.5cm). Make a very narrow double-fold hem on the bottom of the skirt.

7   If you are covering buttons, follow the directions on the package that comes with the buttons. From a scrap of combo fabric approximately ½" x 18" (13mm x 45cm), or pieces 6 and 7, make a tube using the stitch and turn method (page 20). Cut the tube into enough pieces long enough to go over your buttons plus 1" (2.5cm).

8   Press fusible interfacing to the wrong side of half of the placket (9) and to the front and back yoke lining (5, 8).

9   Sew the side seams of the front yoke (3) and back yoke (4) together. Repeat with the yoke lining (5, 8). Sew a gathering thread as indicated at each end of the yoke (3, 4). Fold under and press ¼" (6mm) along the bottom edge of the lining. With right sides together, sew the waist edge of the yoke to the waist edge of the lining. Understitch the waist edge.

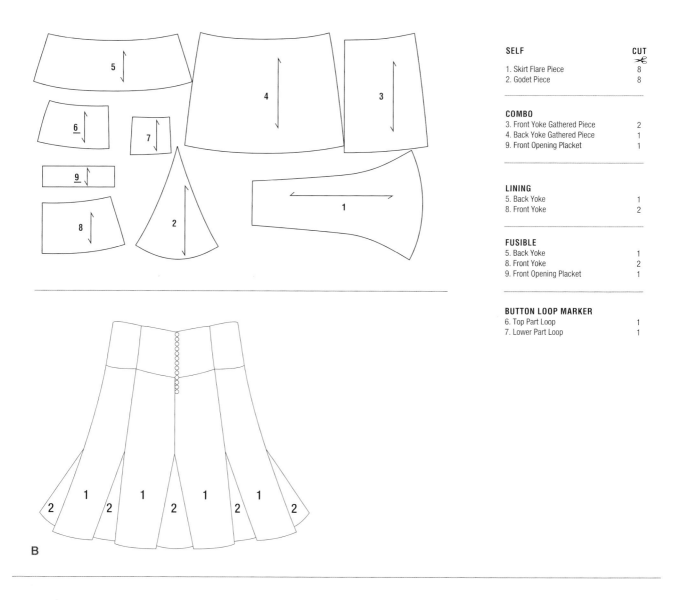

SELF	CUT
1. Skirt Flare Piece	8
2. Godet Piece	8

COMBO	
3. Front Yoke Gathered Piece	2
4. Back Yoke Gathered Piece	1
9. Front Opening Placket	1

LINING	
5. Back Yoke	1
8. Front Yoke	2

FUSIBLE	
5. Back Yoke	1
8. Front Yoke	2
9. Front Opening Placket	1

BUTTON LOOP MARKER	
6. Top Part Loop	1
7. Lower Part Loop	1

B

10 Sew the skirt to the yoke, aligning the side seams. Sewing only through the yoke and not the lining, sew a gathering thread from the top of each gore seam to the top of the yoke.

11 With right sides together, fold the placket (9) in half lengthwise and stitch both ends. Trim corners, turn right side out, and press. Stitch the raw edges together with a ¼" (6mm) seam allowance. Finish the raw edges of the placket with a serger or zigzag stitch. With the raw edges of the placket even with the raw edge of the lining and the top edge of the placket at the top edge of skirt, baste the placket to the right side of the left edge of the yoke lining. Note: The placket is about 2½" (6.5cm) longer than the yoke lining. The excess will be sewn to the skirt in step 13. **(A)**

12 Evenly space the buttonhole strips on the right-hand side of the opening and baste them in place. The raw edge of the buttonhole strip should be even with the raw edge of the lining and the raw edge of the skirt. Approximately 8 strips will be basted to the right-hand side of the yoke lining and 5 to the right-hand side of the skirt. On the inside of skirt, cover the buttonhole strip ends with about a 6½" (16.5cm) length of ¼" (6mm) single-fold bias tape and sew the tape down.

A

13 Gather the yoke edges at the center opening to fit the lining. With right sides together, sew the front edges of the lining and the yoke together.

14 Clip the corners and turn right side out. From the right side, sew the bottom edge of the yoke in the ditch (page 16), catching the bottom edge of the lining in the seam. There will be excess chiffon yoke fabric from the gathers; pin it out of the way so that it doesn't get caught in the seams.

Finishing Touches

15 Evenly distribute the gathers along each gathering line on the yoke. Stitch the yoke to yoke lining on top of each gathering thread.

16 Sew the buttons to the yoke and skirt just inside the placket by following the button loop marker (6, 7) for button loop and button placement.

JAZZ HALL

PAGE 36

This skirt has four flounces. Flounces differ from ruffles in that the top edge of a flounce is fitted exactly to the bottom of the skirt (whereas a ruffle is simply gathered to fit). To avoid bulkiness and to create better drape and movement, only two of the flounces are sewn to the skirt; the other two are sewn to the lining.

SKILL LEVEL   EASY

MATERIALS

2 yd (1.8m) wool tricot (self)

⅞ yd (80cm) same-weight fabric in a contrasting color (combo)

¾ yd (70cm) lining or lightweight rayon fabric

¼ yd (23cm) fusible interfacing

Matching thread

7"–9" (18cm–23cm) invisible zipper

1 hook and eye

seam allowances

½" (13mm) for the side seams; ⅜" (9.5mm) to attach the flounces to the skirt and lining

1   Select the pattern size according to your hip measurement plus 2"–4" (5cm–10cm) ease. Lay out the pattern pieces on the corresponding fabrics, fitting them on the fabric however works for you, and cut. Don't forget to watch the grain lines.

2   Press fusible interfacing to the wrong side of the waistband (3).

3   Baste the side seams of the skirt front (1) and the skirt back (2) together. Baste the back darts. Leave a 7" (18cm) opening on the left side at the waist edge. Try on the skirt. Pin the zipper opening together. Adjust the darts and seams for a perfect fit; make the same adjustments to the lining pieces.

4   Sew the darts as adjusted in the skirt back (2) and the skirt lining back (7).

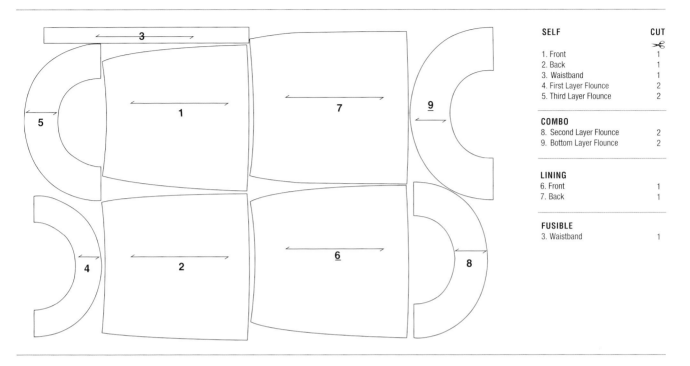

SELF	CUT
	✂
1. Front	1
2. Back	1
3. Waistband	1
4. First Layer Flounce	2
5. Third Layer Flounce	2

COMBO	
8. Second Layer Flounce	2
9. Bottom Layer Flounce	2

LINING	
6. Front	1
7. Back	1

FUSIBLE	
3. Waistband	1

5 Using your favorite method or following the directions on the package, sew the zipper in the left side seam. Finish sewing the left side seam. With right sides facing, sew the skirt's right-hand side seam together.

6 With right sides together, sew the back lining (7) to the front lining (6), leaving a zipper opening in left-hand seam.

7 Match each pair of semicircular flounces (4, 5, 8, 9) by color and size. With the right sides together, stitch the straight side seams. Trim the bottom edge of each seam allowance by cutting a small diagonal from the bottom of the seam to the side of the seam allowance.

8 If desired, finish the bottom edge of each flounce with a ¼" (6mm) double-fold hem. Note: Two flounces are sewn to the skirt and two are sewn to the lining. The red skirt flounce (4) is 3½" (9cm) wide and the cream skirt flounce (8) is 4½" (11cm). The red lining flounce (5) is 4½" (11cm) and the tan lining (9) is 5½" (14cm). With right sides facing up, place the red skirt flounce (4) on top of the cream skirt flounce (8) and baste them together along the top unfinished edge (the inside of the ring). Baste the two lining flounces (5, 9) together along the top unfinished edge.

9 Putting the right sides together, sew the basted edge of the two skirt flounces to the bottom of the skirt with a ⅜" (9.5mm) seam allowance, aligning the side seams. Note: Theoretically, this should be a perfect fit. However, fabric has some give; you may need to make a few clips in the seam allowance or adjust the side seams of the flounce slightly. **Important:** Put the wrong side of the lining flounces (5, 9) to the right side of the lining. Sew the basted edge of the lining flounces to the bottom of the lining using a ⅜" (9.5mm) seam allowance and aligning the side seams.

Finishing Touches

10 Insert the lining into the skirt with wrong sides together, aligning the side seams and zipper opening. Baste the lining to the skirt around the waist edge. Slip stitch the lining to the zipper tape.

11 Attach the waistband to the top of the skirt using the stitch in the ditch method (page 16), setting the front end of the waistband flush with the zipper so the back of the waistband overlaps it by about 1" (2.5cm). Finish the waistband overlap with an invisible slip stitch. On the waistband, sew a hook and eye at the zipper opening (the eye should be on the extension).

CASUAL CHARM
raglan
SLEEVE

Picture New York in the early fall: It's a sunny day and you're walking in Washington Square Park, kicking at the red and gold leaves on the ground. It's not quite cold enough for your trench, but it's not warm enough for just a T-shirt either. Enter the raglan sleeve, a perfect shape for in-between seasons.

02

The tops, tunics, and dresses in this chapter all reimagine this relaxed sleeve at varied lengths and volumes on contemporary shapes. With its loosened silhouette and sometimes full shape, the raglan is one of the prettiest sleeves around, so you might be surprised to learn that it has rather macabre roots. Back in 1855, tailors took their inspiration for this simple-to-sew sleeve from coats made to fit the first Baron Raglan, who had lost his arm after being wounded in the Battle of Waterloo.

You'll be most familiar with raglan sleeves on your baseball sweaters and trench coats, but these days designers use them on shirts, tunics, and babydoll dresses too. Poor Baron Raglan deserves our gratitude, because his eponymous sleeve is super flattering, especially for those with well-defined shoulders, and the diagonal lines also complement feminine curves. Plus, raglan sleeves do not have the typical shoulder seam, so the fit creates freedom of motion and is much more relaxed.

CONTRASTS

If you're drawn to all things femme, you'll love this silk chiffon top with its sexy scoop neckline. The different shades of turquoise will wake up your wardrobe. Be brave and pair it with an airy, abstract-print miniskirt. Once you've mastered this top, try remaking it into a classic sixties-inspired cropped top. To do this, choose wool coating fabric and change the neckline piping to a 1" (2.5cm) band. Then lengthen the sleeves by 8" to 9" (20.5cm–23cm), and switch the bottom piping for a 1" (2.5cm) blind-stitched hem.

TWINKLE TIP
Take it one step further and transform this top into a babydoll tank dress. Just elongate the body by 12" to 14" (30.5cm–35.5cm) and it's yours.

Instructions on page 74.

ON THE SIDE-LINES

Don't fret if frothy romantic styles are not for you. This sportswear-inspired top—a perfect partner for your favorite pair of jeans—will keep you warm and stylish at the same time. We've made this top from a light cocoa sweatshirt fabric. The boatneck is modernized by large buttons, and rivets add a touch of glam to the pockets. Take this top in a feminine direction by wearing it over a floaty skirt.

TWINKLE TIP
For rivets and eyelets, you'll need a grommet tool. Sewing stores usually carry these simple nail tools for around five dollars, or search the Internet for one. Hold onto it after you've made your top— it's also great for embellishing simple belts and leather bracelets.

Instructions on page 77.

BUDDING

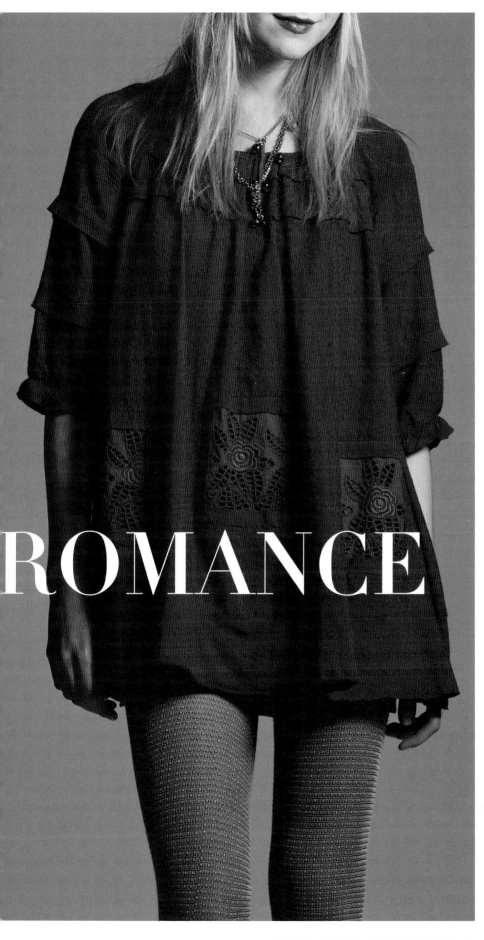

ROMANCE

Enrich your wardrobe with a wine hue in the form of this feminine babydoll shape. I used a merlot-colored blend of rayon, cotton, and wool and added tone-on-tone lace inserts to create an unexpected but gorgeous texture. Piece out the sleeve and add folds or hems to pack it with additional personality. Finish the sleeve by twisting its border. Balance the look with gray tights, chic black heels, and a heavy-knit beanie for additional bohemian flavor.

TWINKLE TIP
Redesign this top by cutting away the seam allowance between the sections on the pattern and taping them together to make a one-piece sleeve instead. Next, eliminate the lace inserts and the frames around them so you have a clean and simpler body. Pipe the neckline and remove the lining. Try this simpler version in a wild-print cotton poplin, and accessorize with flat sandals and large bangles for a perfect beach look.

Instructions on page 80

EYE FOR AN EYELET

Dressing between seasons is a snap with this scoop-neck, raglan-sleeve top that's somewhere between a blouse and a jacket. In a black wool and cotton–blend eyelet, this wardrobe-friendly piece grows out of girlie charm and graduates into sheer sexiness. Wear it with summery pastels like these mellow shades of yellow, which suit almost every complexion. Or choose silk charmeuse and add beading along the neckline to turn this versatile piece into a cocktail cardigan. The same pattern in a wool fabric equals a cool cropped jacket.

Instructions on page 84

TAKE MANHATTAN

Ever have those days when you feel like you have nothing to wear? This relaxed tunic with cropped sleeves, a cowl neck, and a kangaroo pocket is made in a surprisingly dressy men's fabric— a heavyweight mini-basket-weave viscose-and-linen blend—and could be the answer to your wardrobe woes, especially for work. Wear it over a long-sleeved T-shirt and pair with heavy tweed trousers.

To take this tunic to its logical next step, lengthen it by 2" to 3" (5cm–7.5cm) and you'll have a chic tunic dress. In a thick wool, tweed, or herringbone it will look great as a minidress worn over a sweater and colored tights. Try it in a printed silk charmeuse for a fun weekend top to wear over skinny jeans.

TWINKLE TIP
If you choose not to line your tunic, be sure to use French seams at the neckline and the raglan seams, and a rolled hem at the sleeve opening.

Instructions on page 86.

ORIGAMI BLOUSE

When it comes to sleeves, volume remains big news—just observe these bell shapes. The folds on the neckline and sleeves of this tunic resemble Japanese origami, adding terrific texture. Keep the bottom of your outfit simple with solid-hued wide-leg trousers to let this top make a statement. Transform the blouse into a chic evening dress in cream silk charmeuse with a black silk charmeuse tie by simply elongating the body by 12" to 14" (30.5cm–35.5cm).

Instructions on page 89.

71

INSTRUCTIONS

& technical notes

1.

2.

A typical raglan sleeve has a seam that goes on a diagonal from the underarm to the neckline. The sleeve often has a front and back piece sewn together with a seam over the top of the shoulder. The shaping is in the seams. It is possible, however, to make a raglan sleeve in one piece: In this case a dart (or pleats) from the neck to the top of the shoulder pro-

vides the shaping. Since the fit of a raglan sleeve is relaxed, the same size sleeve fits a wide range of shoulder shapes. They are also easy to put in, unlike set-in sleeves, which require easing a curved sleeve to a straight armhole. As you will see from this collection, the sleeves vary in length, from almost no sleeve in Cool Contrasts to long sleeves in On the Sidelines.

In general, the front half of the sleeve is sewn to the front of the garment, the back half of the sleeve to the back, and then the front and back of the sleeve and garment are sewn together. The two pieces then are sewn together in one seam on each side from the bottom of the body to the end of the cuff.

3.

4.

5.

6.

COOL CONTRASTS

This pretty little top, made from three shades of the same color, has a scoop neckline both front and back. The neckline and hem piping are covered with black net that adds delicate, sexy details. The hardest part of this top is deciding which three colors you want. After that, it is a snap to put together. Mark your pieces so you will know which piece you want where.

SKILL LEVEL   EASY

MATERIALS   1 yd (1m) solid-colored silk chiffon for sleeves, lining, and front and back middle panels (self)

1/2 yd (45.5cm) each of 2 complementary colors silk chiffon (combos 1 and 2)

1/2 yd (45.5cm) fancy nylon net or lace (combo 3)

Matching thread

1 yd (1m) self-made double-fold bias tape

seam allowances

3/8" (9.5mm) throughout

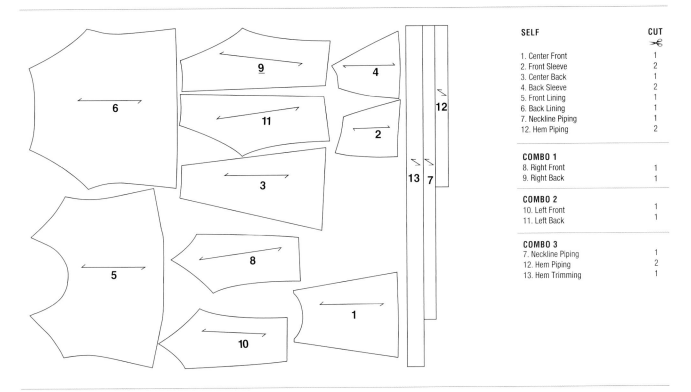

SELF	CUT ✂
1. Center Front	1
2. Front Sleeve	2
3. Center Back	1
4. Back Sleeve	2
5. Front Lining	1
6. Back Lining	1
7. Neckline Piping	1
12. Hem Piping	2

COMBO 1	
8. Right Front	1
9. Right Back	1

COMBO 2	
10. Left Front	1
11. Left Back	1

COMBO 3	
7. Neckline Piping	1
12. Hem Piping	2
13. Hem Trimming	1

1   Select the pattern size according to your bust measurement. Add 1"–2" (2.5cm–5cm) for extra ease. This is a loose-fitting top with plenty of ease, so it is better to choose the next size up rather than the next size down. Lay out the pattern pieces on the corresponding fabrics, fitting them on the fabric however works for you, and cut. Don't forget to watch the grain lines.

2   In the seam allowance, mark the front, back, top, bottom, and the wrong side of each piece. If you have chosen a see-though chiffonlike fabric, mark the seam allowance with a little piece of tape rather than a marking pencil, which might show through. Be sure to use tape that won't leave glue on the fabric when removed!

3   Lay the front and back garment pieces out in order on the table as suggested in **(A)**.

4   With right sides together, sew the front (1, 8, 10) seams together and then the back (3, 9, 11) seams together. With right sides together, sew the front and back together at the side seams.

5   Because these sleeves (2, 4) are not lined, and possibly see-through, finish the sleeves first at the shoulder and underarm by joining with a French seam. Hem the sleeves with a very narrow double-fold hem; your sewing machine may have the perfect presser foot for this kind of hem. With right sides together, baste the sleeves to the front and back, matching the underarm seams.

6   Make darts in the front lining (5) where indicated. With right sides together, sew the lining front (5) and back (6) pieces together along both sides.

7   With right sides together, insert the garment into the lining. Pin the top edges together, matching the sleeve seams. Note: The darts on the lining front should align with the seam lines of the bodice front. Sew the lining and the top together only along the sleeve seams. Clip the point where the side seam and the sleeve seam meet. Remove the pins, and turn the garment right side out.

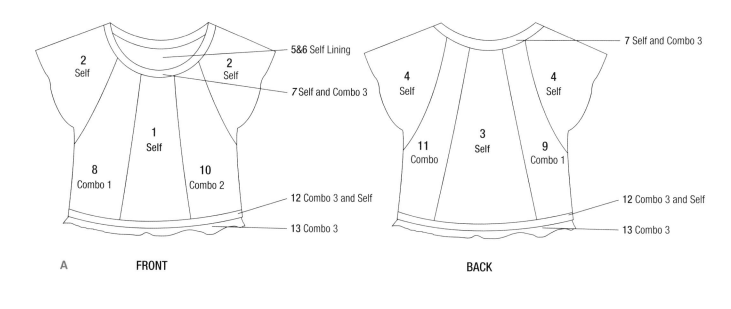

2 Self

2 Self

5&6 Self Lining

7 Self and Combo 3

1 Self

8 Combo 1

10 Combo 2

12 Combo 3 and Self

13 Combo 3

A   **FRONT**

7 Self and Combo 3

4 Self

4 Self

11 Combo

3 Self

9 Combo 1

12 Combo 3 and Self

13 Combo 3

BACK

Finishing Touches

8 Pin the garment and the lining neck edges together. Repeat with the bottom edges.

9 Hand-baste the neckline piping net (7) and the neckline piping strip (7) together on each long edge and treat as one (neckline piping). With the net side out, press the neckline piping in half lengthwise. With right sides together and the raw edge of the neckline piping flush with the neckline, sew the neckline piping to the top edge with a ½" (13mm) seam allowance. Fold the neckline piping to the wrong side of the neck. Fold the seam allowance to the inside. Pin the neckline piping from the outside of garment in the ditch (page 16), being careful to catch the folded seam allowance of the neckline piping on the underside. Secure the neckline piping to the garment by stitching in the ditch. Note: Start about 1" (2.5cm) from one of the side seams, leaving a 2" (5cm) tail of neckline piping. Sew to within 1" (2.5cm) of the starting side seam, then trim the neckline piping, leaving a 2" (5cm) tail. Adjust the ends of the neckline piping for a perfect fit, sew the ends together, and trim the seam to ¼" (6mm).

10 Sew the ends of the net hem trimming together with a French seam. With raw edges together, baste the net hem piping (12) to the hem piping (12) along one long raw edge. **(A)**

Then baste the net hem piping (12) to the hem piping (12) and the trimming (13) along the other long raw edge. Treat as one (hem piping). With right sides facing, sew edge A of hem piping to the inside of the bottom edge of the garment beginning at the side seam. **(B)** Finish the hem piping (12) by stitching in the ditch from the right side of the garment, being careful to catch the hem piping edge in the seam, but not the hem trimming (13).

11 Press the net hem trimming (13) down toward the bottom edge.

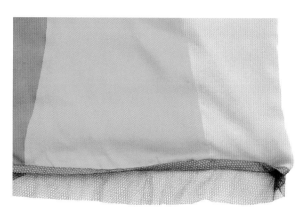

B

This isn't your ordinary sweatshirt. The embellishments of buttons, rivets, and fancy piecing take the ordinary to the extraordinary. I consider the skill level to be advanced because, while sweatshirt fabric is easy to sew, there are many different pieces that fit together like a puzzle. Almost all the seams are topstitched $\frac{1}{16}$" (1.5mm) from the edge for added pocket and neckline finishing.

SKILL LEVEL ADVANCED

MATERIALS

2 yd (1.8m) cotton sweatshirt fabric

$\frac{3}{8}$ yd (34cm) tricot for pocket facing

$\frac{1}{4}$ yd (23cm) fusible interfacing

Thread*

8 rivets or $\frac{1}{2}$" (13mm) buttons

Fabric glue (optional)

1 package matching bias tape

Seven 1" (2.5cm) fancy buttons**

seam allowances

$\frac{1}{2}$" (13mm) for the side seams; $\frac{3}{8}$" (9.5mm) for all other seams

* There is a great deal of topstitching on this garment. You may want to try a contrasting color for extra pizzazz. You can also hand-stitch some of the topstitching for a crafty, artsy look.

** You only need 6 actually, but it's good to have an extra in case you lose a button.

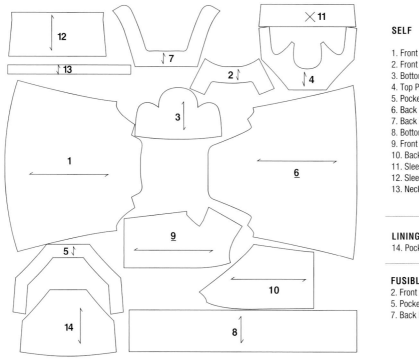

SELF	CUT ✂
1. Front	1
2. Front Neckline	2
3. Bottom Pocket	1
4. Top Pocket	1
5. Pocket Opening	2
6. Back	1
7. Back Neckline	2
8. Bottom Band	1
9. Front Sleeve	2
10. Back Sleeve	2
11. Sleeve Opening Tape	2
12. Sleeve Opening Band	2
13. Neckline Facing	2

LINING	
14. Pocket Facing	1

FUSIBLE	
2. Front Neckline	1
5. Pocket Opening	1
7. Back Neckline	1

1 Select the pattern size according to your bust measurement. Add 1"–2" (2.5cm–5cm) for extra ease. This is a loose-fitting top with plenty of ease, so it is better to choose the next size up rather than the next size down. Lay out the pattern pieces on the corresponding fabrics, fitting them on the fabric however works for you, and cut. Don't forget to watch the grain lines.

2 Press the fusible interfacing to the front neckline (2), the pocket opening (5), and the back neckline (7).

3 Stay stitch all the points on the pocket pieces (3, 4, 5).

4 With right sides together and using a ⅜" (9.5mm) seam allowance, sew the bottom pocket (3) to the top pocket (4). Clip to the points. Clip the curves and trim the corners. Repeat the process to sew the top pocket (4) to the pocket opening (5). Attach rivets or buttons where indicated.

5 With right sides together, sew the second pocket opening (5) to the pocket facing (14). Clip the corners and trim the seam. Turn right side out.

6 Place the right side of the pocket facing to the right side of pocket, and sew the top and the opening edges together.

7 Clip the corners and trim the seams. Turn the pocket right side out. On the side edges of the pocket, press the seam allowances to the inside. Topstitch all the pocket seams except the side seams and the bottom opening.

8 Lay the pocket on the front (1) as indicated, centering and matching the bottom edges. Pin the pocket to the front. **(A)** Topstitch the top and side seams of the pocket to the front of the sweatshirt. Baste the bottom edge of the pocket to the bottom edge of the shirt.

9 Stay stitch along the inside edges of the back neckline facing (13) and the back neckline (7). Reinforce the curves and corners with another row of stay stitches. Clip the curves to the stay stitching and press the seam allowance to the wrong side.

10 With right sides together, sew the outer edge of the back neckline and back neckline facing together (7, 13). Grade the seam, clip, turn, and press. Topstitch the back neckline and facing close to the folded edge. Insert the back (6) between the opening in the neckline pieces just to the depth of the seam allowance. Hint: Glue the back to the facing first, then glue the neckline to the back. This will keep things from sliding around and ensure the back is inserted correctly.

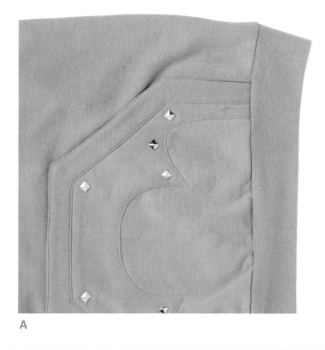

A

B

11 Topstitch around the inside edge of neckline, sewing the back neckline and the back neckline facing together with the sweatshirt back in the middle.

12 Repeat steps 9 and 10 for the front, sewing the front neckline facing (13), the front (1), and the front neckline (2) together. Make 4 buttonholes where indicated.

13 Press the ½" (13mm) seam allowance to the inside on each edge of the facing tab of the front sleeves (9). With wrong sides together, stitch the top edge of the facing together. Press the facing to the inside on the fold line. Topstitch around the edge of the facing, leaving a ¾" (2cm) opening on the inside top edge. Do not sew across the top.

14 With right sides together, sew the front sleeves (9) to the front (1), stopping at the front neckline (2). Sew the back sleeves (10) to the back (6).

15 Fold the bottom of the sleeve opening band (12) to the inside with a 1" (2.5cm) hem. Baste in place. Place the sleeve opening tape (11) on the basting line with ¼" (6mm) of the tape extending toward the fold. **(B)**

16 Topstitch the sleeve opening band (12) over the basting line. Topstitch the other edge of the tape (11) to the band (12) ¼" (6mm) from the top edge of the tape.

17 With right sides of the front sleeves (9) and the back sleeves (10) together, sew both shoulder seams together. Sew bias tape over the seam at the top of the sleeve and the front, tucking the end into the opening on the sleeve facing. Finish topstitching the facing by stitching ¼" (6mm) from the front opening to the back raglan sleeve seam.

18 With right sides together, sew the cuff to the bottom of each sleeve.

19 Sew the underarm and the side seams together as one seam, matching the front and back raglan seam line.

Finishing Touches
20 Sew the short ends of the bottom band (8) together, adjusting the fit to the bottom of the shirt. Fold the band in half lengthwise as indicated, wrong sides together. Pin the open edge of the band flush with the shirt bottom, aligning the band's side seam with one of the shirt's side seams, and stitch in place.

21 Sew on buttons where indicated by the buttonholes on the front neckline and the front sleeve pieces.

I call this sleeve "super raglan" because these are no ordinary raglan sleeves: Each one is constructed from seven pieces. Putting it together will take some time, because there are many design elements to consider. But then, that is part of its charm.

SKILL LEVEL   ADVANCED

MATERIALS

3 yd (2.7m) rayon, cotton, and wool–blend fabric; viscose would also work well (self)

1$\frac{1}{2}$ yd (1.4m) jersey (combo)

Six 6$\frac{3}{4}$" (17cm) cotton lace squares for the inserts (lace combo)

1$\frac{1}{2}$ yd (1.4m) lightweight lining fabric or the same jersey fabric (add another $\frac{1}{2}$ yd [45.5cm] if making your own bias tape)*

$\frac{1}{4}$ yard (23cm) fusible interfacing

Matching thread

1 package single-fold bias tape, or make your own from the lining fabric

seam allowances

$\frac{1}{2}$" (13mm) throughout unless otherwise indicated

* The lining shows through the lace inserts, so be sure to pick a matching or appealing contrasting color.

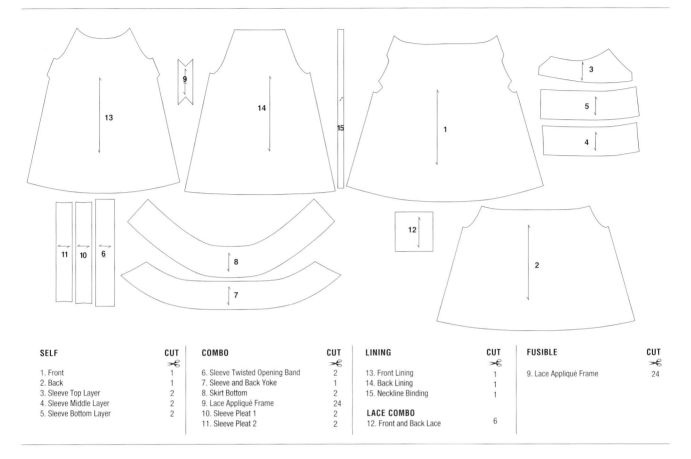

SELF	CUT ✂	COMBO	CUT ✂	LINING	CUT ✂	FUSIBLE	CUT ✂
1. Front	1	6. Sleeve Twisted Opening Band	2	13. Front Lining	1	9. Lace Appliqué Frame	24
2. Back	1	7. Sleeve and Back Yoke	1	14. Back Lining	1		
3. Sleeve Top Layer	2	8. Skirt Bottom	2	15. Neckline Binding	1		
4. Sleeve Middle Layer	2	9. Lace Appliqué Frame	24				
5. Sleeve Bottom Layer	2	10. Sleeve Pleat 1	2	**LACE COMBO**			
		11. Sleeve Pleat 2	2	12. Front and Back Lace	6		

1 This is a very loose-fitting garment; select the pattern size according to your bust measurement plus 1"–2" (2.5cm–5cm) of extra ease. Lay out the pattern pieces. Be sure to mark the wrong side of each pattern piece and the top and bottom of the sleeve pieces. Number each piece in the seam allowance before you cut. Some of the pieces are almost the same; trying to figure out which is which after you cut may be a challenge.

2 Cut out the pattern pieces. Don't forget to cut out the squares for the lace inserts from the front (1) and back (2) where indicated.

3 Press fusible interfacing to all lace appliqué frame pieces (9). There should be 24 pieces for the frames of the lace.

4 For the lace inserts, sew 4 lace appliqué frames (9) together with a ¼" (6mm) seam allowance: Sew along the V at the end of the pieces, pivoting at the point. When the 4 pieces are sewn together, you will have a frame or box. Fold the frame in half with the wrong sides together and press.

5 Lay the frame on the lace square (12) and baste the raw edges together. Stay stitch a scant ⅜" (9.5mm) from the raw edge of the square openings on the front (1) and the back (2). Reinforce the corners with another line of stay stitching. Clip the corners to the stay stitching, being careful not to cut through the stitching. Turn the seam allowances to the inside and press them against the wrong side.

6 With the right side of the lace square to the right side of the square opening seam allowance, but on the wrong side of the front (1) or back (2), sew the squares to the opening seam allowances on the front (1) and back (2). Hint: When going around the corners, leave your needle in the fabric to make the turn, and stitch on the reinforcing line. You might even want to backstitch before and after each corner to make the seam stronger. Repeat steps 4–6 for each lace square.

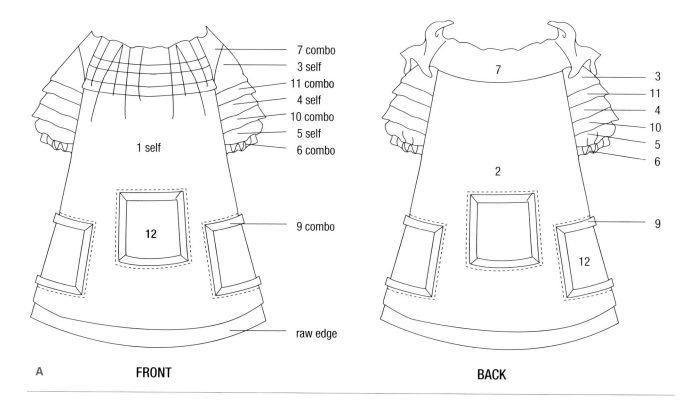

7 combo
3 self
11 combo
4 self
10 combo
5 self
6 combo

1 self

12

9 combo

raw edge

A **FRONT**

7

3
11
4
10
5
6

2

9

12

BACK

7 To sew the sleeves, collect pieces 3, 4, 5, 6, 10, and 11. Before you sew them together, line the pieces up from top to bottom in this order: 3, 11, 4, 10, 5, 6. Fold sleeve piece 10 in half lengthwise as indicated, wrong sides together. Stitch the raw edges of piece 10 between the top of piece 4 and the bottom of piece 3 by laying the raw edge of 10 on the top raw edge of 4 and then laying the bottom raw edge of 3 on top, right sides together. Fold sleeve piece 11 in half lengthwise as indicated, wrong sides together, and sew it between the top of piece 5 and the bottom of piece 4, right sides together. Press the seams down. **(A)**

8 Sew the underarm sleeve seams together, matching the seams of the different pieces. Sew the ends of piece 6 together. Fold the wrong sides of piece 6 together as indicated, sliding the edges in opposite directions so that the cuff is slightly twisted. Baste the open edges together. With a few tiny gathers here and there, pin the cuff to the sleeve bottom with right sides together. Stitch in place. Finish the seam with a serger or zigzag stitch.

9 Sew the back seam of the raglan sleeves to the back (2). With rights sides together, sew the back-shoulder yoke piece (7) to the top of the back and the sleeve piece. **(A)**

10 On the top of the front (1), make horizontal pleats by folding on the lines indicated, pressing, and stitching on the lines. **(B)**

11 Press the pleats down. With right sides facing, sew the front (1) to the front of the sleeves.

B

12 With right sides facing, sew the front and back side seams together. Sew a gathering line around the neckline ⅜" (9.5mm) from the edge.

13 Sew the darts in the front lining (13). Press down. Sew the front lining (13) and the back lining (14) side seams together. Finish the lining with a ½" (13mm) double-fold hem. With the right sides together, insert the lining into the garment and stitch the lining only along the raglan sleeve seams, on top of existing stitches.

14 Clip the seam allowance where the side seam meets the sleeve seam. Turn the garment right side out. With wrong sides together, baste the neck edge of the lining to the neck edge of the garment, adjusting the gathers between the marks as indicated.

Finishing Touches

15 Finish the neckline edge with bias tape.

16 Sew the side seams of the skirt bottom (8) together with a French seam. With right sides together, sew this piece to the bottom of the garment. There is no need to finish the hem of piece 8, unless the fabric you have chosen frays; if it does, make a very narrow double-turned hem.

EYE FOR AN EYELET

This quick little top can be put together in a few hours—start after lunch and wear it to dinner. It features raglan sleeves and a tight waistband. The buttons go on the left front opening extension, and the buttonholes go on the right front opening extension.

SKILL LEVEL   EASY

MATERIALS

1 yd (1m) wool and cotton–blend eyelet (self)

1/2 yd (45.5cm) matching cotton for facings (combo)

1/4 yd (23cm) fusible interfacing

Matching thread

1 package double-fold bias tape, or make your own

1 package single-fold bias tape

Four 3/4" (2cm) and one 1" (2.5cm) fancy buttons

3 yd (2.7m) of 1/4" (6mm) elastic

seam allowances

1/2" (13mm) for side seams and armhole sleeves; 3/8" (9.5mm) for all others

1   Select the pattern size according to your bust measurement plus 1"–2" (2.5cm–5cm). Before you cut out the waistband, check the size against your waist and adjust the band accordingly. There is a slight gather on the front and back bodice pieces, so you can easily make the waistband either larger or smaller. Lay out and cut the pattern pieces.

(Note: You will need to cut twice as many combo pieces [2, 4, 7] because one set is fused and used as a facing, and the other set serves as an interfacing to block the holes of the eyelet fabric. This method is also used in the sleeve opening band [8].)

2   Press fusible interfacing to one combo set of pattern pieces 2, 4, and 7.

3   For the button band and the buttonhole band, baste the second set of combo pieces 2 to the fused side of combo facing pieces 2. Press the seam allowances toward the inside on the inside edge of the front opening extension (2). With right sides together, sew the front opening extension facing (2) to the band along center front line.

4   With right sides together, stitch the front opening extension (2) to the front (1). Repeat for both front opening extensions.

5   Using French seams, sew the front sleeve (3) and the back sleeve (6) together at the shoulder and underarm seams. Make an elastic casing at the bottom of each sleeve with narrow-fold bias tape. **(A)**

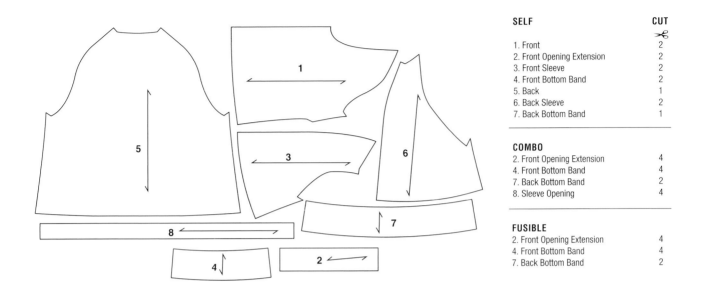

SELF	CUT ✂
1. Front	2
2. Front Opening Extension	2
3. Front Sleeve	2
4. Front Bottom Band	2
5. Back	1
6. Back Sleeve	2
7. Back Bottom Band	1

COMBO	
2. Front Opening Extension	4
4. Front Bottom Band	4
7. Back Bottom Band	2
8. Sleeve Opening	4

FUSIBLE	
2. Front Opening Extension	4
4. Front Bottom Band	4
7. Back Bottom Band	2

6 Sew the darts on both front (1) pieces where indicated. Press down. Using French seams, sew the front (1) and back (5) side seams together. With regular seams and right sides together, sew the sleeves to the jacket, matching the underarm and the side seams. Cover the armhole seam allowances with the double-fold bias tape. Finish the neck edge with single-fold bias tape.

7 With right sides together, sew the combo front opening extension to its facing at the top edge. Clip the corner, grade the seam, and turn right side out. Press along the fold line. Fold and press the facing seam allowance to inside. Stitch in place by stitching in the ditch (page 16) on the seam line of the front opening extension (2) and front (1). Be sure to catch the neck edge bias tape in the seam.

8 Sew the side seams of the front (4) and back (7) bottom bands together. Repeat on the combo bottom band facing and the bottom band interfacing (4, 7). With wrong sides together, baste the bottom band interfacing to the bottom band facing. With right sides together, sew the combo bottom band facing to the bottom band along the bottom edge. Press a ⅜" (9.5mm) seam allowance on the top of the facing to the inside.

9 Stitch the right side of the bottom band to the right side of the garment along the bottom edge, matching the side seams. Understitch the seam. Stitch the ends together, clip the corners, grade the seam, and turn right side out. Stitch the band facing to the garment by stitching in the ditch (page 16). Hint: The process is the same as putting on a waistband, except it is upside down.

Finishing Touches

10 Make 1 horizontal buttonhole at the neck edge, 1 in the waistband, and 3 evenly spaced vertical buttonholes on the right front. Sew the buttons on the left front band, placing the larger 1" (2.5cm) button at the bottom.

11 Measure a piece of elastic to fit your arm plus 1" (2.5cm). Insert elastic in the sleeve casings. Overlap the ends and stitch to secure.

A

This overblouse is the easiest of the garments in this chapter to put together. The cowl collar comes with a tie that gives flexibility to your style. If you choose not to line the top, use French seams for the neckline, the raglan seams, and the sleeve opening.

SKILL LEVEL EASY

MATERIALS

2 yd (1.8m) viscose and linen–blend fabric

³/₄ yd (70cm) medium-weight rayon or lining fabric

¹/₂ yd (45.5cm) fusible interfacing

Matching thread

2 rivets or ¹/₂" (13mm) buttons (optional)

1 package single-fold bias tape

seam allowances

¹/₂" (13mm) for the side seams; ³/₈" (9.5mm) for all other seams

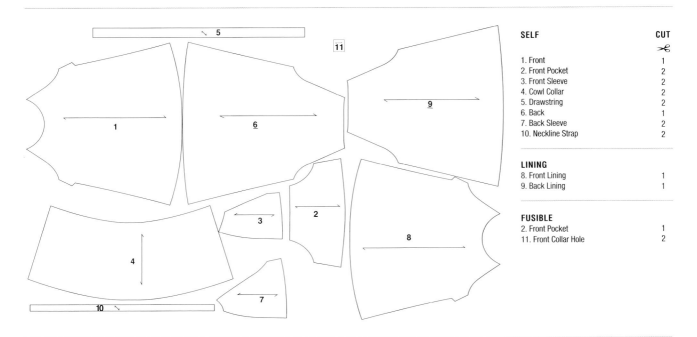

SELF	CUT
	✄
1. Front	1
2. Front Pocket	2
3. Front Sleeve	2
4. Cowl Collar	2
5. Drawstring	2
6. Back	1
7. Back Sleeve	2
10. Neckline Strap	2

LINING	
8. Front Lining	1
9. Back Lining	1

FUSIBLE	
2. Front Pocket	1
11. Front Collar Hole	2

1   Select the pattern size according to your bust measurement. This is a loose-fitting garment with a slight A-line shape. Allow for extra ease to form the tank shape when selecting your size. Lay out the pattern pieces on the corresponding fabrics, fitting them on the fabric however works for you, and cut. Don't forget to watch the grain lines.

2   Press fusible interfacing to the front collar hole.

3   With rights sides together, sew the two pocket pieces (2) together, leaving a small opening for turning. Clip the curves, snip the corners, and grade the seam. Turn the pocket right side out. Press the seam allowance at the opening to the inside and slip stitch. Topstitch the curved edges (the pocket openings) ¼" (6mm) from the edge. Pin the pocket to the front (1) where indicated. Topstitch the pocket very close to the edge along the top, sides, and bottom, leaving the curved edges open. Topstitch two vertical lines ¼" (6mm) apart down the middle of the pocket. (This decorative stitching will keep the pocket from gaping open.) Embellish the top corners of the pocket with optional rivets or buttons.

4   Sew the darts on the front (1) and front lining (8) and press them down. With right sides facing, sew the front and back (1, 6) together at the side seams. Repeat with the front lining (8) and the back lining (9).

5   Put the lining and the garment wrong sides together, matching the sleeve lines and side seams. Baste the wrong side of the lining to the wrong side of the tunic along the raglan seam lines and neckline.

6   Sew the front sleeve (3) and the back sleeve (7) shoulder seams and underarm seams. Make a 1" (2.5cm) hem on the bottom of the sleeves. I finished the bottom edge with a serger (you can pink the hem instead) and made a 1" (2.5cm) single-fold blind-stitched hem.

7   Sew the sleeves to the front and back of the garment. Clip the seam allowance at the point where the sleeve seam meets the side seam.

A

8 On one cowl collar piece (4), find the center front point on the longer curved edge. To each side of this point, make a buttonhole approximately 1½" (3.8cm) from the center point and just slightly more than ½" (13mm) in from the edge; the buttonhole should be about ½" (13mm) long. **(A)** Sew the back seam on each collar piece. With right sides together and aligning the back seams, sew the collar pieces together around the longer curved (non-neck) edge using a ½" (13mm) seam allowance. Grade the seam, turn right side out, and press.

9 With wrong sides together, topstitch ½" (13mm) from the longer curved edge to form a casing for the tie. Be careful to keep the buttonholes centered in the casing.

10 With wrong sides together, baste the neck edges of body and collar together, aligning the center front point and the back seams. Sew the collar to the top of the garment with a ⅜" (9.5mm) seam allowance. Clip and grade the seam. Sew bias tape to the inside neck edge, covering the seam allowances.

Finishing Touches

11 Make a drawstring tie (5) using either the fold and stitch method (page 20) or the stitch and turn method (page 20). Thread the tie through the casing using a small safety pin or a turning tool. To keep the tie from slipping out, tack it down to the casing on the back seam.

ORIGAMI BLOUSE PAGE 71

The neckline of this top looks complicated but is actually very easy. The raglan sleeves are pleated around the neck edge to add additional styling. Finish off with a contrasting tie and you are ready for fun.

SKILL LEVEL   ADVANCED

MATERIALS

1 yd (1m) cotton shirting fabric (self)

$^1/_4$ yd (23cm) cotton jersey in a contrasting color (combo)

$^1/_4$ yd (23cm) fusible interfacing

Matching thread

$^1/_2$ yd (45.5cm) of $^1/_4$" (6mm) elastic

1 package single-fold bias tape

seam allowances

$^1/_2$" (13mm) for the side seams; $^1/_4$" (6mm) for the hem; $^3/_8$" (9.5mm) for all others

1   Select the pattern size according to your bust measurement plus 1"–2" (2.5cm–5cm). Lay out the pattern pieces on the corresponding fabrics, fitting them on the fabric however works for you, and cut. Don't forget to watch the grain lines.

2   Press interfacing to the wrong side of the neckband extension (6).

3   The sleeves (3) do not have a shoulder seam; the shape is created by the neck-edge pleats. Pin the pleats in place as marked. Sew the pleats down about $^1/_2$" (13mm) in from the pleat fold line. Sew the underarm seams together. **(A)**

4   On the bottom edge of the sleeve, sew a 9" (23cm) of elastic to the inside 1" (2.5cm) from the bottom edge. Fold the sleeve to the inside 1$^1/_2$" (3.8cm) from the bottom edge, turn under $^1/_4$" (6mm) and stitch down.

5   Baste the pleats in place at the neck edge of the back (2). Finish the neck edge with bias tape.

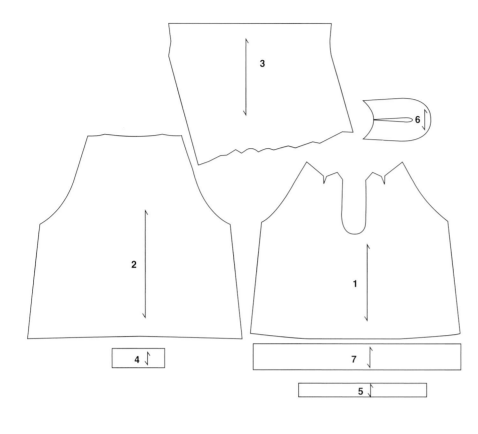

SELF	CUT ✂
1. Front	1
2. Back	1
3. Sleeve	2
4. Origami Embellishment	8
5. Front Neckline Trim	2

COMBO	
6. Neck Band Extension	2
7. Front Neck Ties	2

FUSIBLE	
6. Neck Band Extension	2

6 Baste the pleats in place at the neck edge of the front (1). Finish with bias tape. Stay stitch the outside and inside curve of the front neckline extension (6) and the front (1) center neckline curve. With right sides together, sew the front neckline extension facing (6) to the front neckline. on the inside edge. Sew the outside curve of the front neck extension to the front neck opening (1). Clip and grade the seam. Understitch. With the seam allowance folded in, stitch the facing down, using the stitch in the ditch method (page 16). Sew the 8 origami embellishments (4) to the front neck opening. **(B)** Press unsewn points of the rectangles down to meet bottom edge of the rectangle.

7 Sew the front (1) and back (2) side seams together with French seams.

8 Sew the sleeves to the front and back, matching underarm and side seams. The top of the front and back pieces should meet the pleat stitching on the sleeves. Clip the seam allowance at the intersection of the side seam and the raglan seam. Finish the top of the sleeve with a serger or zigzag stitch. Fold the top of the sleeve to the inside 1¼" (3cm) and hand-stitch the edge to the sleeve. Be careful not to catch the top of the pleats in your stitching. When folding and readjusting the ends of the pleated sleeve top, be sure to cover the ends of the bias tape on both the front and back.

Finishing Touches

9 Make the ties (7) using the stitch and turn method (page 20). Finish the ends and press flat. Topstitch each tie along the front neck edge (around all four sides, including the neck opening), with the end of the tie about ⅜" (9mm) from the shoulder seam line and tucked under the pleat.

10 Hem the garment with a very narrow double-fold hem.

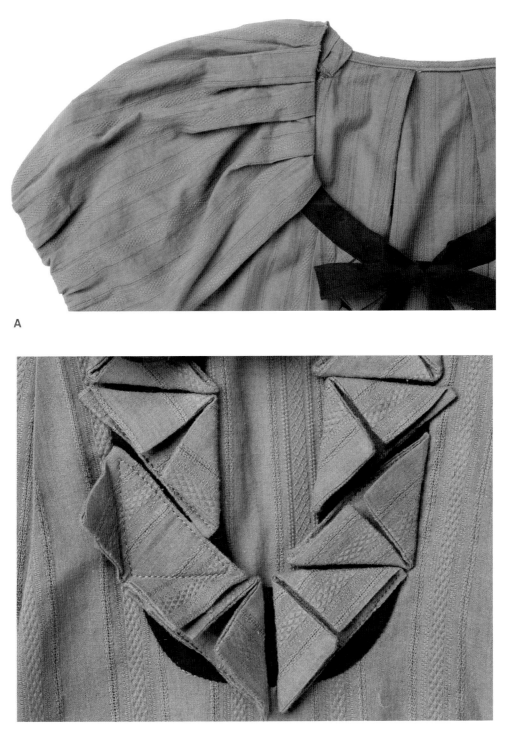

A

B

drop SHOULDER

Throughout history, designers have used clothing to change the proportions of the body. And when it comes to sleeves, we've seen shoulders modified by everything from regal puffed-up Victorian leg-of-mutton shoulders to less stuffy peasant styles.

03

In the sixties, the drop shoulder made a comeback inspired by the youthquake. Dresses that looked like they belonged on little girls had puffed sleeves and hems three or four inches (7.5cm–10cm) above the knee. In recent seasons, loose volumes and baby-doll proportions have looked fresh and right once more. The drop-shoulder sleeve adds a romantic touch to these effortless tent dresses and tunics. Drop-shoulder sleeves are easy to wear—in Queen Victoria's time, women played croquet or went to the beach in a garibaldi blouse featuring this more relaxed shape. These days they are part of the uniform seen on chic, arty girls at gallery openings in Chelsea.

I like to think that my drop-shoulder designs are sexy in a nontraditional way.

There are various shapes of drop shoulders in this chapter. Some tops, such as White Magic and the Next Big Thing, have no sleeve at all, although those without sleeves still have a sleeve-shaped cover from the drop of the shoulder, which I think is the most flattering sleeve shape of all. It covers the upper arm and under-arm but at the same time gives a garment a summery, sleeveless look. Many pieces, such as Boy Meets Girl and Balancing Act, have a relaxed silhouette in the form of a babydoll or loose tunic. One thing I usually try to avoid is a shapeless man's shirt, but looking sexy in an oversize shirt can be achieved. The Balancing Act blouse, for instance, has quirky boyish details, while Boy Meets Girl has a jazzy tuxedo flavor.

BOY
MEETS
GIRL

Work a masculine-feminine look with this tuxedo-inspired shirt. But instead of staying with the traditional penguin palette of black and white, stand out in the crowd with this dark gray version with a black bib. This boxy blouse has many interesting details—an asymmetrical bib, pleats, a little bow tie, and sleeve tabs. They play with the menswear-inspired theme and add a sense of humor. There are many pattern pieces, but patience rather than expert skill is required. The best part of home sewing is creating a labor-intensive, delicate garment that would normally cost you $1,500. This way, you can spend your television time creating something you will be proud to wear, while saving money at the same time.

The lightweight cotton has subtle dobby details, which add texture to the simple shape. The look is sexy with a coolly ambiguous twist. Cinch your supersized blouse with a belt for a glamorous look, or wear it over black skinny jeans. Tuck it into a pair of Marlene Dietrich–style wide-legged trousers with oxford shoes, or, if you like to show off your gams, add opaque tights and ankle boots.

TWINKLE TIP
For something sexier shorten
the sleeves, lengthen the shirt
by 6" (15cm), and tell the penguins
that all is forgiven by choosing
white and black silk charmeuse.

Instructions on page 108.

DARK SECRETS

This darkly romantic top, in polka-dotted black silk chiffon, will surprise you with its simplicity. This is one of the easiest projects in this chapter, though you'd never think it, what with the ribbon-crossed yoke embellished with rivets. Whimsical polka dots bring a French flair, while the single layer of sheer chiffon along the neckline accentuates the ribbon grid. Wear with a gray pencil skirt at the office or let it top a sleek pair of tuxedo pants for evening.

If you are not making this piece in chiffon, try to play with contrasting colors or fabrics that will highlight the yoke. Choose shirting fabric in white and navy, for example, to create a nautical feel. You can easily create a fun summer dress by elongating the length by 10" (25.5cm), changing the fabric to cotton voile, and substituting the chiffon yoke with eyelet or another contrasting fabric. For a chic babydoll dress, simply elongate the shirt by 12" (30.5cm).

Instructions on page 111.

BALANCING ACT

This boyish shirt looks great on girls, especially when paired with culottes and brogues. The diamond pleats add gorgeous texture to this gray go-anywhere top. I chose a viscose-and-linen blend, but for a crisp Jackie O–inspired look, try it in a striped shirting fabric, white shirting fabric, or blue oxford cloth.

These pleats are not difficult to make, but the skill requires patience. Carve out the time (and maybe find an episode of *Project Runway* to watch), and you can do them in front of the television. Once you've mastered this pleating, you will be ready for the more challenging pleating and smocking to come. This is also a good opportunity to hone your piping skills.

TWINKLE TIP
For a preppier look, substitute the diamond pleats with simple pin tucks.

Instructions on page 114.

NEXT BIG THING

This sexy balloon-skirted dress in modern silver is an ideal replacement for the little black dress and perfect for a night on the town. For a more nostalgic look, choose jewel-toned ombré silk. The unique neckline is knotted to resemble a necklace—adorn it with beads or crystals for an additional sparkly effect.

TWINKLE TIP
Turn this into an evening dress by forgoing the balloon shape and making the skirt floor length instead. To lengthen it, elongate the side seam by smoothly following the original side seam. The skirt of the lining should use the exact same pattern as the new elongated skirt shell.

Instructions on page 118.

POETRY IN MOTION

Slinky, slouchy, and chic: In luxurious silk-and-viscose velvet, this is the most comfortable minidress around. Is it day or evening? It doesn't matter. Wear it over black leggings and knee-high riding boots and you can work it both ways. The dip neckline with sheer crinkled-chiffon pleats and draped collar adds a regal, sophisticated element to this simple tunic. For a different feel, try replacing the chiffon with lace or a contrasting color. If you've fallen for this uncomplicated, boxy shape, consider making a couple of these tops in different fabrics. For a breezy resort look, for instance, try white eyelet or tropical-print cotton. For a sixties-inspired modern look, make the jumper in heavy wool tweed or brocade and wear it over a geometric-print blouse with tights and a pair of flats.

TWINKLE TIP
For a boxy shift, remove the sleeves completely. Reshape the armholes so the curve naturally blends in with the side seam and remove the pleats around neckline (but keep the draping collar). The result? A sleeveless funnel-neck jumper.

Instructions on page 122.

WHITE MAGIC

If versatility sits high up on your list of fashion requirements, look no further than this flowing tunic dress. I chose an ivory silk-and-wool blend, which is soft and drapes nicely. Try it with skinny jeans and a tank top for spring, wear it free-flowing at a summer picnic, belt it for a cleaner and sexier look, or layer it over a turtleneck sweater for fall. Go white on white by wearing it over a white tank top with white pumps and a white bag, or dress it down by wearing it over one or more differently colored tank tops. Try this dress with a more structured fabric such as wool pinstripe or wool plaid for a cool schoolgirl-meets-slouchy truant look. Wear it with chunky boots and frayed jeans.

Instructions on page 125.

INSTRUCTIONS
& technical notes

1.

2.

3.

As with the raglan sleeve, the seam between the sleeve and bodice does not need to hit at the edge of the shoulder in drop-shoulder tops. The seam can be almost anywhere, from just off the shoulder to the elbow. The advantages? Flexibility in sizing and ease of attachment. It's not quite true that one size fits all, but one size fits a variety of shapes, especially for menswear-inspired garments like Boy Meets Girl, which has a very generous fit. A drop-shoulder sleeve is shaped almost like a rectangle or a trapezoid, which makes inserting it easy because there is very little easing in of a sharp curve to a straight line, which is typical of regular set-in sleeves. It is helpful when cutting out the pattern to mark the center of the top of the sleeve. This mark will match up with the shoulder seam when you finally assemble the garment.

1. Poetry in Motion, 2. White Magic,
3. Boy Meets Girl, 4. Dark Secrets, 5. Balancing Act,
6. Next Big Thing

4.

5.

6.

BOY MEETS GIRL PAGE 94

If you like to keep life interesting by being a little off center, this big lightweight cotton shirt is for you. This complicated oversize blouse has many pieces, but if you follow the steps in order, you'll be having fun in no time.

SKILL LEVEL   ADVANCED

MATERIALS

2 yd (1.8m) lightweight cotton (self)

1 yd (1m) contrasting lightweight cotton jersey (combo)

1 yd (1m) fusible interfacing

Matching thread

1 yd (1m) of $^1/_{16}$" (1.5mm) piping cord

Twelve $^5/_8$" (16mm) buttons

seam allowances

$^1/_2$" (13mm) for the side seams; $^3/_8$" (9.5mm) for all others

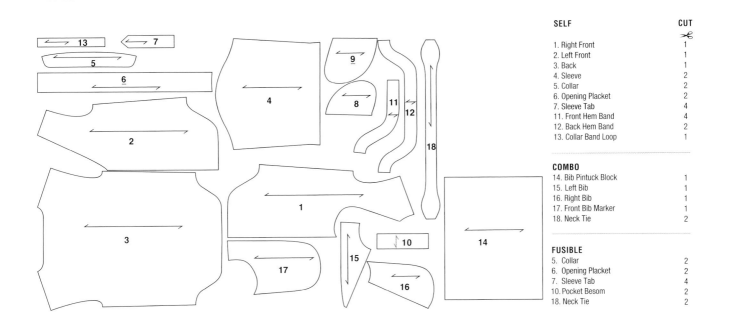

SELF	CUT
	✂
1. Right Front	1
2. Left Front	1
3. Back	1
4. Sleeve	2
5. Collar	2
6. Opening Placket	2
7. Sleeve Tab	4
11. Front Hem Band	4
12. Back Hem Band	2
13. Collar Band Loop	1

COMBO	
14. Bib Pintuck Block	1
15. Left Bib	1
16. Right Bib	1
17. Front Bib Marker	1
18. Neck Tie	2

FUSIBLE	
5. Collar	2
6. Opening Placket	2
7. Sleeve Tab	4
10. Pocket Besom	2
18. Neck Tie	2

1 This is a big shirt with a large amount of ease. It is intended to be loose fitting; select your pattern size accordingly. Lay out the pieces on the corresponding fabrics, fitting them on the fabric however works for you. Prepare pintucks on piece 14 and press tucks all in one direction. Cutting from the prepared pintuck piece (14), cut 1 right front bib and 1 left front bib. Make sure you lay the pattern pieces on the pintucks so that the pintucks end up on the outside of the garment and the right and left sides are correct.

2 Press fusible interfacing on the wrong side of pieces 5, 6, 7, and 10.

3 Make tabs for the sleeves by sewing the tab (7) and tab facing (7) with right sides together, leaving the flat short end open. Clip the corners. Turn the tab right side out and press flat. Make a buttonhole on the pointed end as indicated. Turn the seam allowances on the open end to the inside. Topstitch close to the edge on all sides. Place one tab where indicated on the wrong side of each sleeve (4) and topstitch in place with a boxed X.

4 Sew the underarm seams together with a French seam. Hem the wrist edge of the sleeve. (I topstitched a 1" [2.5cm] hem with a ¼" [6mm] fold.)

5 The right and left bib pieces are shaped differently, but the process of assembling them is the same. With the contrasting jersey, make about 1 yd (1m) of piping. To do this, cut a strip of fabric about ¾" (2cm) wide and 1 yd (1m) long. Fold the fabric with wrong sides together over the piping cord. Using your zipper foot or a cording foot, sew as close to the cording as possible. On the outside edge of the bib pieces, baste the piping to the right side of the pintucked bib pieces (15, 16) with raw edges flush. **(A)**

6 On the front pieces (1, 2), stay stitch the line where the bib and front piece meet. Clip the curve to the stay stitching. Baste the right side of each bib lining piece (15, 16) to the wrong side of the corresponding front piece (2, 1). With right sides together, sew the bib to the bib lining close to the piping. Note: The front of the garment will be sandwiched between the bib and bib lining. Clip the curve. Turn the bib so the wrong sides of the bib and bib lining are together and the right side of shirt front faces away from the facing. Press flat. With wrong sides together, baste the top of the facing and front edge of the bib together.

7 Baste the pleats indicated at the collar edge of the back (3). Sew the front (1, 2) and the back (3) together at the shoulder seams and the side seams. (For a polished finish, make French seams.)

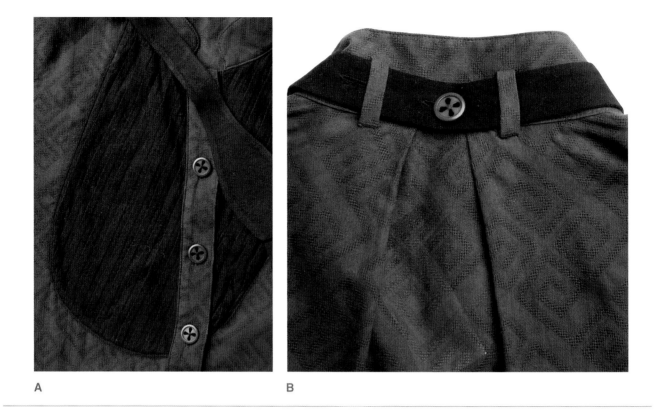

A   B

8 Sew the back hem band (12) and front hem band (11) together at the side seams. Repeat with the front and back hem band facing (11, 12). With right sides together, sew the bottom edge of the hem band facing and the hem band piece, matching seam lines. Trim and clip the seam. Turn right side out and press. With wrong sides together, top-stitch very close to the bottom edge of the trim. Baste the top of the hem band and the top edge of the hem band facing together. If you have a serger, serge the hem band to the bottom of the shirt. Press the seam allowance down, and topstitch close to the seam line. If you do not have a serger, sew the hem band to the bottom edge of the shirt as you would put on a waistband, using the stitch in the ditch method (page 16).

9 With wrong sides together, press the center front fold on the opening placket (6) where indicated. Stitch the placket (6) to the shirt front as you would a waistband, using the stitch in the ditch method. Topstitch close to the edge all the way around the bands of the placket.

10 Sew the sleeves in place. You may need to ease in the sleeve at the shoulder seam a small amount.

11 Make the 4 collar band loops (13) ½" x 2" (13mm x 5cm) using the stitch and turn method (page 20). Hint: Make a tube from the collar band loop (13) slightly longer than 8" (20.5cm), then cut it into 4 equal-length pieces. On the outside collar (5), tack the collar loops where indicated on the pattern. With right sides together, sew the collar facing (5) to the collar (5) along the top edge, being careful not to catch the loops. Trim and clip the seam. Turn the collar right side out and press. Stitch the collar to the neckline as you would a waistband using the stitch in the ditch method. Topstitch around the edges of the collar.

12 Make the neck tie (18), following the instructions for making a tube with the stitch and turn method. On the neck tie, make a buttonhole where indicated. **(B)**

Finishing Touches

13 Make 9 vertical buttonholes on the front right band of the placket (6) where indicated. Sew buttons on the left front band, the center back of the collar, and on the right side of the sleeve where the tab was sewn. By hand, tack the loose end of the loops for the necktie to the shirt.

This drop-shoulder top has a ribbon grid yoke accentuated with rivets. If you don't have a rivet attachment machine, buttons will work just as well. The simple sleeves have puffy balloon bottoms, which look difficult but are a breeze to sew in. This top slips on easily with only one button and no zippers. You don't have to line this garment if you choose a more opaque fabric.

SKILL LEVEL   EASY

MATERIALS

1 yd (1m) silk chiffon

1 yd (1m) silk chiffon or crepe for lining

Matching thread

7 rivets or $^3/_8$" (12mm) buttons

1 package double-fold bias tape (optional)

1 button for back neck opening

seam allowances

$^1/_4$" (6mm) for the back keyhole; $^3/_8$" (9.5mm) for all others unless otherwise indicated

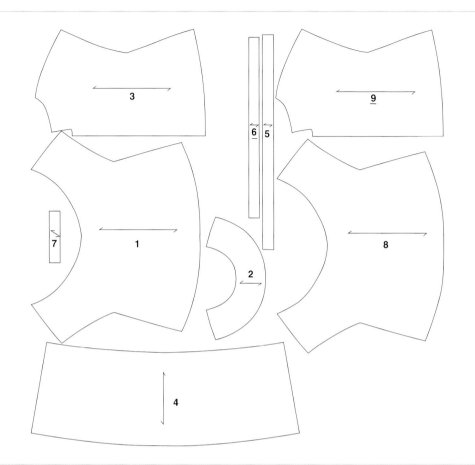

SELF   **CUT**

1. Front   1
2. Neckline Yoke   1
3. Back   2
4. Sleeve Opening   2
5. Neckline Piping   1
6. Neckline Tape   2
7. Back Button Loop   1

LINING

8. Front Lining   1
9. Back Lining   2

1 Select the pattern size according to your bust measurement. Lay out the pattern pieces on the corresponding fabrics, fitting them on the fabric however works for you, and cut. Don't forget to watch the grain lines.

2 Make neckline piping (5) for the front yoke using the stitch and turn method (page 20). Press the strip flat. Cut one long strip and seven short strips according to the guide on the neckline yoke (2). Lay strips on the guide (2). Attach rivets or sew buttons at intersections. With the wrong side of the yoke-strip embellishment to the right side of the neckline yoke (2), baste the strips in place along the top and bottom edge of the neckline yoke (2).

3 Sew a gathering thread by hand or machine along the top edge of the front (1) between the markings. Pin the front (1) to the yoke (2), adjusting the gathers to fit. Sew the yoke to the front on top of the gathering thread.

4 Make the back button loop (7) using the stitch and turn method, and baste it to the top edge of the right-hand back neck opening (3). (An alternative to sewing the loop is to make one from very narrow elastic.) Sew the center back (3) seam to the mark for the keyhole opening. **(A)**

5 Sew the front (1) and back (3) together at the side seams and the shoulder seams. Finish the bottom hem with a ¼" (6mm) double-fold hem.

6 Sew a gathering thread either by hand or machine along both longer edges of the balloon sleeve (4). Sew the underarm sleeve seams (4) together. Fold the rectangular sleeve piece in half, wrong sides together, aligning to the diagonal lines on the pattern and creating a twist in the fabric. Adjust the gathers to fit. Pin the raw edges together and carefully sew another gathering thread on top of the previous one. The balloon will be twisted; don't try to straighten it out! **(B)**

A

B

7 With right sides together, attach the balloon sleeve to the armhole opening in the front and back pieces, matching the underarm seams. Adjust the gathers to fit the armhole. Sew the balloon sleeve in place on top of the gathering stitches.

8 Sew the back seam of the lining (9) to the mark for the keyhole opening. Sew the front lining (8) and the back lining (9) side seams together. Finish the lining with a ¼" (6mm) double-fold hem.

9 Insert the garment into the lining, right sides together, matching all seams. Pin in place. Note: The lining only goes to the bottom of the yoke in the front. Sew the back-neck keyhole opening with a ¼" (6mm) seam allowance. Under-stitch. Sew a gathering stitch to the top edge of the lining, and gather the lining to fit the yoke. Sew the lining to the bottom of the yoke on the front (2), to the shoulder seams,

and to sleeve openings (4) on top of the previous stitches. Do not sew the neck edge. Clip the seam where sleeve and side seam intersect and on any curved edges. Turn the garment to the right side. Baste the back neckline of the lining and the garment together.

Finishing Touches

10 Encase the neck edge in a bias strip of the same fabric (6) (or double-fold bias tape) as if it were a waistband, using the stitch in the ditch method (page 16).

11 Sew the button to the right back neck edge.

This gray button-down features several unique embellishments, from the diamond-pleated yoke insert to the binding ribbons on the collar and sleeves. This blouse is easy to wear but a little tricky to put together. The sleeve-opening finish is a little like origami: You have to make your folds in the right directions or your bird may end up looking like an elephant. Don't get discouraged, though; with a little patience you'll have it ready to go in no time.

SKILL LEVEL   ADVANCED

MATERIALS

1 1/2 yd (1.4m) viscose, polyamide, and linen–blend fabric

1/2 yd (45.5cm) lightweight fusible interfacing

Matching thread

1 package bias tape

Six 5/8" (16mm) buttons

seam allowances

1/2" (13mm) the side seams; 3/8" (9.5mm) for all others

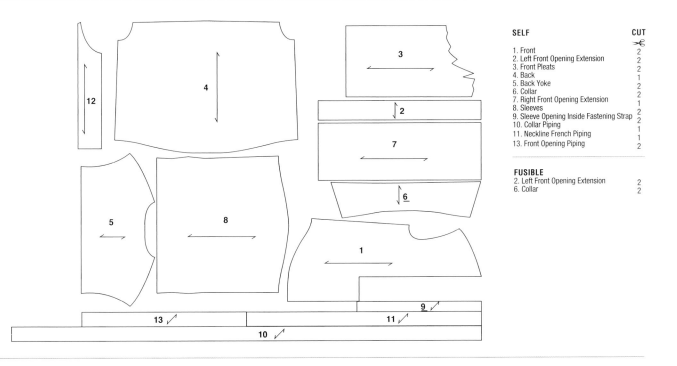

1 Select the pattern size according to your bust measurement. Lay out your pattern pieces, fitting them on the fabric however works for you, and cut. Don't forget to watch the grain lines.

2 Press fusible interfacing to the collar lining (6) and the left front opening extension (2).

3 Using pattern pieces 10, 11, and 13, prepare the piping. Cut the length of collar piping (10) into 3 sections—50" (127cm), 5" (12.5cm), and 5" (12.5cm). For the collar piping, use the stitch and turn method (page 20) to make a tube approximately 14" (36cm) long from both ends, leaving the center of the strip open the length of the collar edge. Finish both ends before turning tubes right side out. Prepare all other trim piping as if it were double-fold bias tape. For the sleeve ties (9), use the stitch and turn method.

4 Sew the pleats on piece 3 following the lines on the pattern. Press the pleats flat so that the middle of the pleat falls directly over the seam line. From the wrong side, use the stitch in the ditch method (page 16) on the seam lines so that the pleats are sewn through the center. **(A)**

5 On the first and third pleats and, starting 3" (7.5cm) from the bottom of the insert, machine stitch horizontally just across the pleat, backstitching 1 stitch on each edge of the pleat, every 3" (7.5cm). On the middle pleat, starting 1½" (3.8cm) from the bottom of the insert, stitch horizontally across the pleat every 3" (7.5cm).

6 Reinforce the inside corner of each front (1) opening piece with stay stitches. Clip to the point. With right sides together, sew the pleated insert (3) to the front (1), pivoting at the point. Be careful not to catch any of the pleats in the stitching. Reinforce the corner by stitching over previous stitches.

7 On the top center of the back (4), baste the pleat as marked. With the right side of the back yoke (5) to the right side of the back (4), stitch the bottom of the back yoke (5) to the back (4). Sew the front (1) to the back yoke (5) at the shoulder seams.

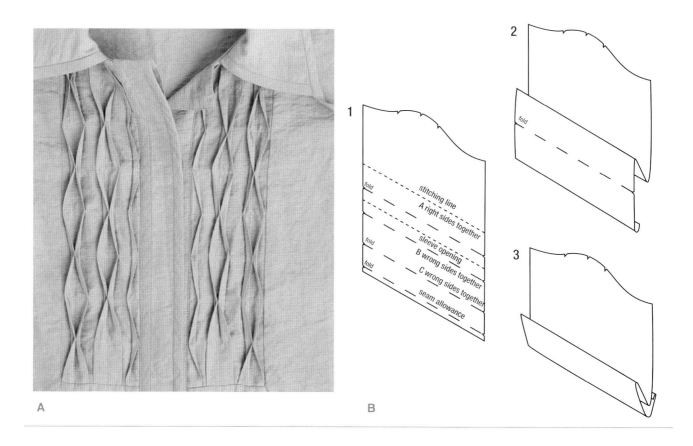

A

B

8 On the back yoke facing (5), press the seam allowance under on the shoulder seams. With the right side of the yoke facing the wrong side of the shirt back and the yoke pointing down, sew the bottom of the yoke facing to the back on top of the previous seam stitches. Press the yoke facing up. Pin the yoke facing to the yoke at the shoulder seams as if to stitch in the ditch. From the right side, stitch in the ditch of the shoulder seams, making sure to catch the yoke facing in the seam.

9 Leaving the underarm seam of the sleeve and the side seams of the blouse open, sew the sleeve (8) to the front (1) and back (4, 5). Sew the side seam and the underarm seam, from the bottom of the shirt to the sleeve opening in one seam.

10 Follow the folding directions in (B). Press each fold at the end of the sleeve in place before even thinking about stitching. Open the sleeve out. It's OK if the hem fold doesn't want to open out. Sew the sleeve tie (9) to the bottom of the sleeve where indicated with raw edges even. Pin the tie so that it doesn't get caught in the other seams; you'll just have to keep pushing it out of the way. Refold on the A fold with right sides together. Sew a line of stitching 1½" (3.8cm) from the fold line. Refold on the B fold. Wrong sides will be together. Keep folding. Refold on the C fold. The C fold will be covering the A fold. With D folded, from the right side of the sleeve, pin the D fold by pinning in the ditch of the first stitching line. You will have to hold the B fold back out of the way. Stitch in the ditch, catching the D fold in the stitching.

11 Finish the hem of the blouse with a ¼" (6mm) double-fold hem.

12 With wrong sides together, baste the collar (6) and under-collar together on all sides. Sew the shorter piping pieces on each end of the collar as you would any double-fold tape, using the stitch in the ditch method. In the same manner as putting on a waistband using the stitch in the ditch method, attach the open center of the long piping strip (10) to the outer edge of the collar. With the under-collar

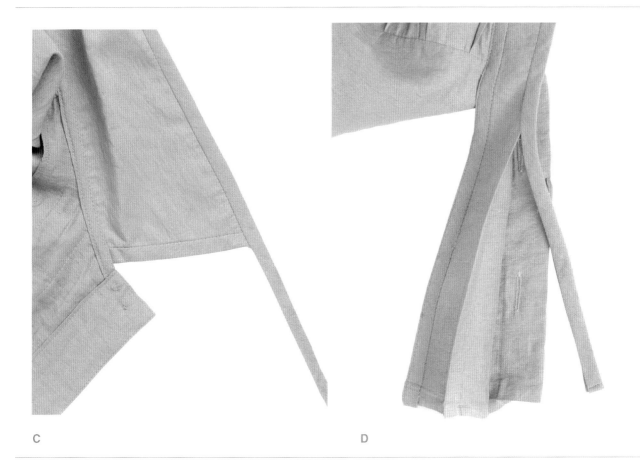

C

D

facing the right side of the shirt, baste the collar to the neckline of the shirt. Using neckline piping (11), sew one edge of the piping to the collar on top of the previous stitching line, extending the piping past the ends of the collar to the front opening. Grade the seam and clip in several places. Topstitch the open edge of the piping to the neck edge, enclosing all the seam allowances and sewing though all of the layers. (C)

13 To make the left front button band, with right sides together, stitch the left front opening extension (2) to the left button band, leaving the left edge open. With right sides together, sew just the button band to the left front (1). Sew across the bottom and top of the band. Clip the corners and turn the band right side out. Press the seam allowances of the button band facing to the inside. Pin the band in place, neatly tucking in all the ends. Topstitch close to the edge around the entire band, being sure to catch the button band facing in the seam.

14 The right front opening extension (7) requires more origami folding. Hint: Label each fold with a tiny safety pin and a tag. Make 6 buttonholes as indicated between fold A and fold B where marked. Cover fold D and the left raw edge with folded front opening piping (13). Turn fold B back on itself and stitch across the top and bottom of the band. Refold B back to its original position, tucking in the ends. Slip the right front edge of the shirt ⅜" (9.5mm) in between folds A and C. Topstitch only the inside edge of the band, securing the front edge between the folds. (D)

Finishing Touches

15 Tack the front left band together along the open edge between the buttonholes. Tack the pleats on the insert to form a diamond pattern. Pinch the pleat together and hand stitch as close as possible to the edge with 1 or 2 tiny stitches.

16 Sew on the buttons. Tie the collar ribbons to the sleeve ribbons.

This balloon-skirted dress has dropped its sleeves entirely. The dress plays a little trick to get away with its boxy shape: To shape the bodice, a seam has been added along the side seam between the underarm and waistband for a few inches. The neckline requires neat sewing to shape each curve and corner perfectly and evenly while inserting the knotted strap at the center of each curve. If you are new to sewing, you might want to start with one of the easier designs in this collection.

SKILL LEVEL ADVANCED

MATERIALS

1¹/₂ yd (1.4m) cotton, viscose, and polyester–blend fabric

1¹/₂ yd (1.4m) lining fabric

¹/₄ yd (23cm) fusible interfacing

Matching thread

15" (38cm) invisible zipper

20" (51cm) of 1" (2.5cm) elastic

seam allowances

¹/₂" (13mm) for the side seams; ³/₈" (9.5mm) for all others

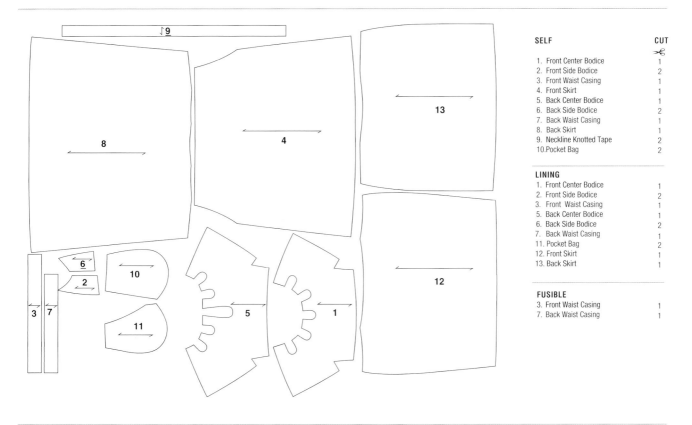

SELF	CUT
	✄
1. Front Center Bodice	1
2. Front Side Bodice	2
3. Front Waist Casing	1
4. Front Skirt	1
5. Back Center Bodice	1
6. Back Side Bodice	2
7. Back Waist Casing	1
8. Back Skirt	1
9. Neckline Knotted Tape	2
10. Pocket Bag	2

LINING	
1. Front Center Bodice	1
2. Front Side Bodice	2
3. Front Waist Casing	1
5. Back Center Bodice	1
6. Back Side Bodice	2
7. Back Waist Casing	1
11. Pocket Bag	2
12. Front Skirt	1
13. Back Skirt	1

FUSIBLE	
3. Front Waist Casing	1
7. Back Waist Casing	1

1 Select the pattern size according to your bust measurement. Lay out the pattern pieces, fitting them on the fabric however works for you, and cut. Don't forget to watch the grain lines.

2 Press fusible interfacing to the front (3) and back (7) waist casing.

3 Sew the pocket bag lining (11) to the edge of the front skirt (4), matching the raw edges of the waist and the side seams. Understitch. Sew the pocket bag (10) to the pocket bag lining (11), right sides together. Baste the pocket to the skirt at the waist and side edges, matching the marks.

4 On the front center bodice (1), reinforce the point between the sleeve and front with stay stitches. Clip to the point. With right sides together, sew the front side bodice (2) to the front center bodice (1), pivoting at the point. Repeat with the front side lining (2) and front center lining (1) pieces. Sew the bottom edge of the front center bodice (1)

to the top of the front waist casing (3) with right sides together. Sew the top of the lining casing to the bottom of the lining bodice with right sides together. Repeat with the back bodice (5, 6), bodice lining, and back waist casings (7).

5 To make the bottom, sew a gathering stitch along the top of the front skirt (4). Adjusting the gathers to fit, pin and then stitch the top of the skirt (4) to the bottom of the front waist casing (3). Sew a gathering stitch along the bottom of the back side bodice (6). Make pleats in the back skirt (8) where indicated and baste. Sew the back skirt (8) to the bottom of the back waist casing (7).

6 Using your favorite method or following the directions on the package, insert an invisible zipper into the left side seam, beginning about 1" (2.5cm) from the edge of the sleeve at the underarm; finish sewing the top and bottom of the left seam. Sew the right side seam together, matching the seams where the casings meet.

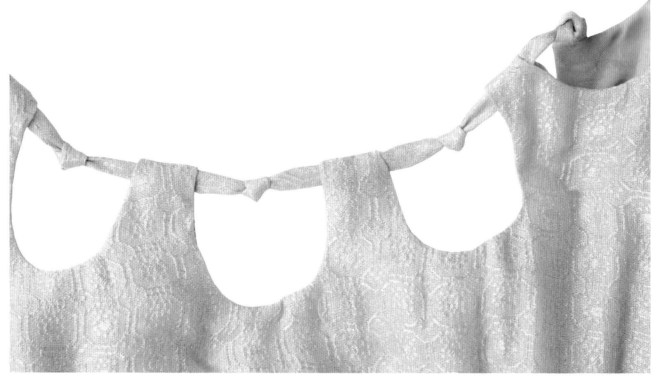

A

7 Sew the front (1) and back (5) bodices together at the shoulder seams. Sew the front (1) and back (5) lining bodices together at the shoulder seams. With the right side of the lining to the right side of the bodice, pin the lining in place along neckline. Sew across the tops of the scallops at the neckline. Sew the lining to each scalloped edge, including the back opening. Leave about ½" (13mm) open at the top edge of each side of the scallops for the tie. Sew the underarm seams of the lining together. Trim and clip all the curves. Turn the bodice right side out. Press the seam allowance of the bodice and lining on the sleeve openings to the inside. Very close to the edge, topstitch the lining to the garment at the sleeve opening. Understitch the lining.

8 Sew the top of the casing lining in the same seam as the top of the bodice and casing seam.

9 To make the balloon skirt, sew the right-hand side seam of the front (12) and back (13) skirt lining. Sew the left side seam together, leaving the top open for the zipper. Sew a gathering thread around the bottom of the skirt and also around the bottom of the skirt lining. Slightly gather the bottom of the lining. With right sides together and matching the side seams, adjust the gathers on the skirt to fit the skirt lining and pin together. Hint: The skirt is longer than the lining, so some of the skirt will fold up and in to meet the lining. Sew the skirt and lining together, adjusting gathers for a balloon effect. Understitch. Turn the skirt right side out.

10 Baste the pleats in place on the front (12) and back (13) lining where marked. Stitch the top of the lining to the seam of the casing and skirt. Sew the right-hand side seam of the lining casing together. Cut the elastic equal to the length of the front (1) bottom seam. Insert the elastic. Topstitch the elastic through both sides of the casing. Press the seam allowance of the bottom of the casing lining to the inside. From the right side, pin the bottom edge of the casing to the skirt and then stitch in the ditch (page 16), being careful to catch the casing lining in the seam.

Finishing Touches

11 Make a tie from the neckline knotted tape (9) using the stitch and turn method (page 20). Find the center of the ribbon and tie a half knot in it. Thread the ribbon through the scallop points on each side of the center point on the bodice front. Tack the ribbon to the points. Tie a half-knot in the ribbon halfway to the next point. Thread the ribbon through the next point and tack the ribbon to the point. Continue around the neckline. **(B)**

12 Slip stitch the lining to the zipper tape.

This great party dress has a deep front neckline accentuated with a crinkled silk chiffon cowl collar and ruffled edge. The dropped sleeves are a snap to put in.

SKILL LEVEL   EASY

MATERIALS

1³/₄ yd (1.6m) silk and viscose–blend velvet (self)

³/₄ yd (70cm) crinkled silk chiffon (combo)

1³/₄ yd (1.6m) lining fabric

Matching thread

seam allowances

¹/₂" (13mm) for the side seams; ³/₈" (9.5mm) for all others

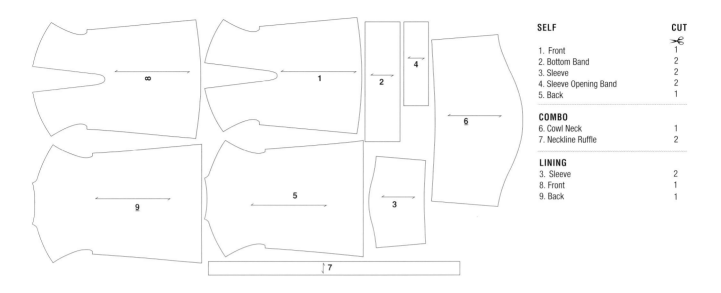

SELF	CUT ✂
1. Front	1
2. Bottom Band	2
3. Sleeve	2
4. Sleeve Opening Band	2
5. Back	1
COMBO	
6. Cowl Neck	1
7. Neckline Ruffle	2
LINING	
3. Sleeve	2
8. Front	1
9. Back	1

1 Select your pattern size according to your hip or bust measurement, whichever is larger. Lay out and cut pattern pieces on the corresponding fabrics, fitting them on the fabric however works for you, and cut. Be sure to mark the center top of the sleeve where it will meet the shoulder seam.

2 With right sides together, sew the shoulder seams and the side seams of the front (1) and back (5). Sew the ends of the bottom band (2) together at the side seams. Fold the band in half lengthwise with the wrong sides together and baste the raw edges together. Serge or sew the band around the right side of the bottom of the dress, matching side seams.

3 With right sides together, sew the sleeve opening band (4) to the bottom of the sleeve (3). With right sides together and matching the band seam, sew the underarm sleeve seams. Sew the sleeves into the garment, matching the underarm sleeve seams with the side seams and the shoulder seams with the sleeve markings.

4 Sew the ends of the neckline ruffle (7) together with a French seam to make a large circle. Finish the bottom edge with a rolled or very narrow hem. (You may have a presser foot that will help with this hem.) Using pins, pleat the ruffle as indicated. Adjust the pleats so that the pleated ruffle fits the neckline. Baste the top edge of the pleated ruffle to hold the pleats in place.

5 Sew the back seam of the cowl (6) together with a French seam. Finish the top (straight) edge with a rolled or narrow hem. About 4" (10cm) on both sides of the center back seam, pleat the cowl horizontally, following the marks indicated. You do not have to be exact. The goal is to make the height of the back of the collar about 4" (10cm). Stitch the pleats in place. **(A)**

6 Pin the pleated ruffle to the right side of the neckline, basted edge flush with the neckline, adjusting the ruffles to make it to fit. Pin the cowl to the garment, raw edge flush with the neckline. You will have a sandwich—right side of garment (1, 5), wrong side of pleated ruffle (7), right side of cowl (the curved side) (6). Be sure to put the center back seam of the cowl at the center of the garment back. Baste all layers together.

A

7 Make the lining by sewing the back lining (9) and the front lining (8) together at the shoulder and side seams, right sides together. Finish the bottom of the lining with a ½" (13mm) double-fold hem.

8 On the sleeve lining (3), sew the underarm seams together. Sew the sleeve lining into the lining, right sides together, matching the underarm sleeve seams with the side seams and the shoulder seams with the markings.

9 With right sides together, sew the lining to the garment around the neck edge, matching seams. There are many layers, so be careful not to get the excess chiffon caught in the seam. (You might want to pin the ruffle and cowl out of the way.) Sew the bottom of the sleeve lining to the bottom of sleeve, aligning the underarm seams. Clip and grade the seams. Turn the lining to the inside.

Finishing Touches

10 With pleated ruffle and cowl out of the way, topstitch the lining and the garment ¼" (6mm) from the neck edge. Be careful not to catch any of the chiffon in the stitching.

11 Slip stitch the lining to the side seams.

WHITE MAGIC

PAGE 104

The focal point of this tunic dress is the pleats at the center front, which create a three-dimensional effect. You can bead between the pleats to accentuate the neckline. The very low back-neck drop gives this tunic a sexy yet sporty feel. It ties at the back of the neck, but you can replace the ties with a fixed band.

SKILL LEVEL INTERMEDIATE

MATERIALS

1 1/2 yd (1.4m) silk and wool-blend fabric

1/4 yd (23cm) fusible interfacing

Matching thread

Elastic thread

6" (15cm) of 1/4" (6mm) elastic

Bias tape

seam allowances

1/2" (13mm) for the side seams;
3/8" (9.5mm) for all others

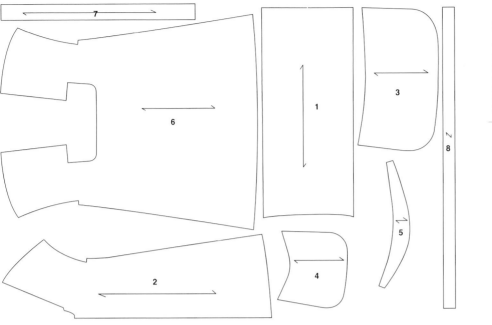

SELF	CUT
	✂
1. Front Center	1
2. Front Side	2
3. Pocket	2
4. Pocket Facing	2
5. Sleeve Opening	2
6. Back	1
7. Back Strap	2

LINING	
8. Hem Binding Tape	2

1   Select the pattern size according to your bust measurement. Lay out the pattern pieces on the corresponding fabrics, fitting them on the fabric however works for you, and cut. Don't forget to watch the grain lines.

2   If using fragile fabric, avoid fraying by pressing strips of fusible interfacing to the top of the front center panel where the pleats are (1) and the sleeve edge (5). Press ⅜" (4mm) under on one long edge of hem binding tape (8).

3   Sew darts in the bottom of the pocket (3) corners as indicated on the pattern. Sew gathering lines along the top and bottom edges of the pockets (3). With right sides together, sew the top and bottom of the pocket facing (4) to the pockets, gathering the pockets to fit. Leave the side seams open. Understitch the top edge. Trim the seams and turn right side out. Pin the pocket (3) to the front side (2), matching raw edges.

4   Baste the sides of the pockets onto the front side panels around the curve (2). Topstitch the bottom of each pocket to the front side panel very close to the edge.

5   Cut the bias tape for the hem binding (8) as indicated. It should be approximately 1½" to 2" (4cm–5cm) shorter than the bottom of the front side panels. Sew a gathering stitch ¼" (6mm) from the bottom of the front side panels. Sew the bias tape to the bottom of panel, adjusting the gathers to fit. Fold the tape to the inside and topstitch close to the folded edge of the tape. This will create a slight puff of the skirt to mirror the puff of the pockets.

6   Sew tiny pleats along the neck edge of the front side panels (2) as indicated. Finish the top edge with bias tape as you did for the hem.

7   Starting ½" (13mm) from the seam line, sew a ¼" (6mm) double-fold hem at the top edge of the center front panel (1), leaving ½" (13mm) open at each end. Sew pleats as indicated. Press the pleats in one direction, but do not sew the tops of the pleats down.

8   With right sides together, sew the front side pieces (2) to the center front piece (1).

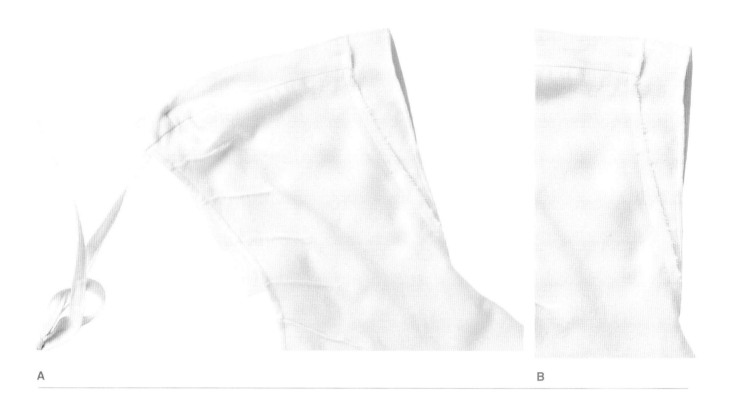

A

B

9 Sew a ¼" (6mm) casing from bias tape to the center of the back (6) neckline between the marks as indicated on pattern.

10 Using elastic thread in the needle, not in the bobbin, sew 9 horizontal lines ½" (13mm) apart across the center of the back as indicated. The uppermost line indicated on the pattern will be the line of stitching from the casing tape. Insert elastic into the casing and secure at both ends.

11 Finish the rest of the back top edge to the left and right with seam binding to ¼" (6mm) from the mark, tucking the loose ends into the casing.

12 With right sides together, sew the front (1, 2) and back (6) together at the side and shoulder seams.

13 With right sides folded together where indicated, sew the bottom of the back facing extension. Trim the corners and grade the seams. Press the outside edge seam allowance and the top seam allowance to the inside. Turn to the right side and press the fold. Topstitch the facing extension

seam allowance to the back, leaving ½" (13mm) open at shoulder seam for the tie. **(A)**

14 Finish the center front and back panels with a double-fold hem that lines up evenly with the rest of the hem edge that has already been finished with binding tape.

15 Finish the sleeve opening (5) with a tiny double-fold hem. Sew the right side of the sleeve to the *wrong* side of armhole, matching the underarm seam. Note: This will create a raw frayed edge on the right side of the garment. **(B)**

Finishing Touches

16 Make the back strap ties (7) using either the stitch and turn (page 20) or fold and stitch method (page 20). Slip the ties under the back extension at the shoulder seams and stitch in place. Slip stitch the top of the back extension in place along the shoulder seam on top of the extension.

PLAYFUL POISE

spaghetti
STRAPS

*All it takes is one of Twinkle's sweetly sexy spaghetti-strap dresses or tops
to transport you to a bench on a boardwalk beneath blue skies.
You have an ice cream cone in your hand and nothing better to do
than stare out at the yachts on the horizon.*

04

Every girl needs a vacation—and a vacation wardrobe. This chapter is about everything that's great to wear in summer, and spaghetti straps are the perfect emblem of summer's casual charm. What could be more lovely than feeling the warm breeze on your bare shoulders as dusk sets in?

All of these projects have their place in a sunny holiday setting, but they will also make you stand out at a relaxed party, or even at the office if you wear them with a blazer or a light cardigan.

Layering is also a great opportunity to play with color and texture of garments and accessories. With some creative combining, these pieces can truly become year-round wear.

Hit a groove of loose, easy loveliness with these sewing projects. Each item is a variation on the camisole shape, in materials that feel light and delicate against the skin. And each has a giggly, sweet femininity–think of of Kirsten Dunst in Sofia Coppola's film *The Virgin Suicides*. You too can now reveal your inner *gamine*!

FLAPPER CAMISOLE

This top would be just another innocently feminine silk camisole if it weren't for the edginess of the multiple straps, fabric strips, and raw edges. The glamorous bias cut, hand beading on the straps, and delicate fraying of the cream, petal, and rose fabric creates a vintage lingerie look. I used crinkled silk chiffon, silk-and-wool gauze, and silk-and-Lycra charmeuse, but there is really no limit to the variety of fabrics to choose from. Stay with solid colors for these strips so the delicate beading and stitching details show.

For a rock 'n' roll look, make it in black and smoky grays. Go for snow white or fire-engine red and you will have a perfect holiday top—just add a sleek skirt and heels. Elongate it to a tunic for a very cool minidress for a springtime Sunday-afternoon party. Dress it down with cotton shorts or jeans—the perfect getup for brunch by the sea. Or dress it up for a night on the town with a pair of cigarette pants and a sharp blazer.

TWINKLE TIP
Instead of beading, add extra edge by topstitching multiple lines in metallic thread.

Instructions on page 142.

CHAMELEON

This flowing dress in silk or cotton voile is my first choice for sashaying along the French Riviera. In cotton poplin, the same frock is perfect for posing poolside in the shade of palm trees. The magic of this dress is in the print, which graduates from light to dark in a vertical direction, and in the design, which is long enough to show the beauty of the print. The secret lies in combining fabrics. The bottom portion picks up the black and adds a coral tone, which in turn is picked up

DRESS

by the peach trim along the neckline. When you choose your fabric, try to find a similar selection. Make sure all the colors blend gradually into one another, or look for a pattern with movement. Whether you go for a dress in comfortable cotton or dressier silk, the satin band at the neckline adds a luxurious touch.

Try it in a lavender-based print with a charcoal and gray combo, or go for spicy colors to brighten it up. For a more dramatic effect, try stripes and cut the skirt on the bias. And if it's romance you're after, try crinkled chiffon in a large floral print over polka dots. Pair with flat, strappy sandals.

TWINKLE TIP
Beads or sequins along the neckline will add glamour to the design. Get a stud fixer and you can create extra glitz by adding stones or studs to the neckband.

Instructions on page 144.

LOVE IN THE AFTER-NOON

With its form-defining topstitching (albeit with a bright, sporty twist), cocoon shape, and origami-inspired detail, this dress can take you from a country club to a cocktail party. The bust band is cut from a wide green stripe and embellished with khaki topstitching. The asymmetrical shoulder straps make an interesting focal point. I chose a striped cotton, but a solid color would be a great backdrop for the frock's shape and would make the origami folds really pop. Make it in ivory eyelet or cotton piqué and wear with Sabrina heels for a cool, ladylike summer look.

TWINKLE TIP
Turn this casual dress into a sexy camisole by shortening it and making it in a black and white geometric-print silk charmeuse.

Instructions on page 146.

CARNIVAL

You're not imagining it: The striped print on this silk charmeuse taps into Twinkle's playful spirit and gives this dress a liquid effect. The fluid ribbon print sets this frock in motion, and the shirred bust and pleated skirt add extra movement. The wonderful lines of the flared silk skirt create a perpetual swirling sensation. This dress is asking to be worn while dancing at a summer soiree—just add beads.

Instructions on page 149.

DRESS

AGE OF INNOCENCE

Mimicking the trend of underwear as outerwear, the nude fabric under the black fabric of this top is a sexy, unexpected optical illusion. Any fabric with good drapability in two contrasting colors will work. Choose solid shades, but mix and match matte and shiny fabrics such as chiffon and charmeuse. By day, dress it down and play the innocent ingenue with khaki cotton shorts, but at night vamp it up with black skinny jeans and high-heeled black sandals.

TWINKLE TIP
Elongate this piece by 4" to 6"
(10cm–15cm) to create a trendy
bubble dress.

Instructions on page 152.

READ BETWEEN THE LINES

Lines play a leading role in this fun top with a mini-jacquard stripe contrasting with a wide black and white bands. The juxtaposition of solid fabric and stripes gives the top a nautical flare. For a different look, choose from a striped fabric, but place the stripes horizontal at the bust and vertical on the hem. Cotton shorts make it yacht-ready, but crisp wide-legged white trousers and wedge sandals will make it office-friendly.

TWINKLE TIP
If you don't want your bra straps to show, wear a plain colored tank underneath.

Instructions on page 154.

INSTRUCTIONS

& technical notes

1.

2.

3.

How many different ways can you flavor pasta? Answer: the same number of ways you can vary spaghetti straps. The tops and dresses in this chapter take the simple spaghetti strap to new design heights. The good news is that they are also very easy to sew. For the most part, spaghetti straps are just tubes of fabric that have been made either with the stitch and turn method (page 20) or the fold and stitch method (page 20). The process is the same whether you are making angel-hair pasta or fettuccini. Once you have decided on the size of the spaghetti straps, let your imagination run wild and embellish, embellish, embellish.

Want some fun? This top is for you. Even though it is easy to make, there are many opportunities for your own creativity to shine through—it's all in the trim. Vary the colors of the deco strips, from subtle shading to bold contrast. And the beading! Go wild! Beading supply stores have almost an infinite number of colors and shapes of beads.

SKILL LEVEL   EASY

MATERIALS

1 yd (1m) silk and Lycra–blend charmeuse (self)

Matching thread

2 each of 2" (5cm) bias-cut strips (about ¹/₂ yd [45.5cm] of each fabric)

of coordinating colors in silk crinkled chiffon, silk-and-wool gauze, and silk-and-Lycra charmeuse (combos 1, 2, 3, and 4). Refer to illustration (B) for each fabric and its corresponding pattern piece.

A variety of matching beads

seam allowances

¹/₂" (13mm) for the side seams; ³/₈" (9.5mm) for all others

1   Select the pattern size according to your bust measurement. When used with a stretch fabric (ours was made in silk-and-Lycra charmeuse), the pattern is roomy enough; if you choose fabric without stretch, you might want to go up a size. Lay out the pattern pieces on the corresponding fabrics, fitting them on the fabric however works for you, and cut. Don't forget to watch the grain lines.

2   With right sides together, sew the side front panels (2) to the center front (1). These are princess seams. If you need to make any size adjustments, these seams are a good place to start. Sew the front (1, 2) to the back (3) at the side seams with right sides together. (Here is another place to make some minor size alterations.)

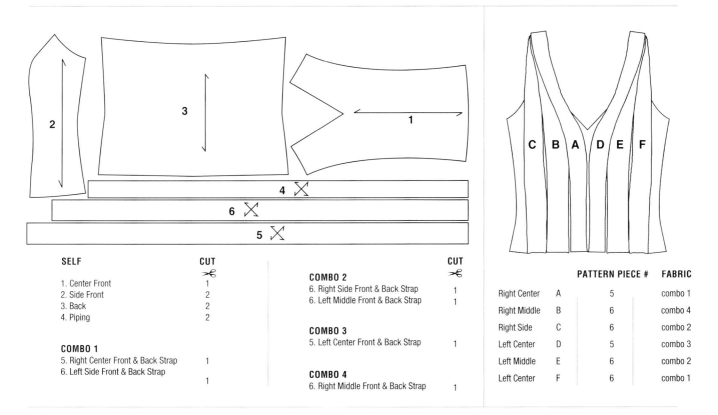

SELF	CUT ✂
1. Center Front	1
2. Side Front	2
3. Back	2
4. Piping	2

COMBO 1

	CUT
5. Right Center Front & Back Strap	1
6. Left Side Front & Back Strap	1

COMBO 2	CUT ✂
6. Right Side Front & Back Strap	1
6. Left Middle Front & Back Strap	1

COMBO 3

5. Left Center Front & Back Strap	1

COMBO 4

6. Right Middle Front & Back Strap	1

		PATTERN PIECE #	FABRIC
Right Center	A	5	combo 1
Right Middle	B	6	combo 4
Right Side	C	6	combo 2
Left Center	D	5	combo 3
Left Middle	E	6	combo 2
Left Center	F	6	combo 1

3 Hem the garment with a ½" (13mm) double-fold hem.

4 For the spaghetti shoulder straps, make bias tape from the piping piece (4) and attach it from one top point of the bust around the back neckline to the top point of the bust on the other side using the stitch in the ditch method (page 16).

5 For the front bias tape (4), measure the length from the center front neckline to the top point of the bust. Then measure the length from the top point of the bust to the back neckline, adjusting the length for your body. You will need two straps of this second length, but don't cut yet. Note: If you make the straps too small at the start, you will have to start over. It is better to make them longer and cut off what you don't need later. The total length of bias you need will be the length of the shoulder straps beyond the neckline piping all the way to the back, plus the front armhole and cross back neckline piping. This is made in one piece. From each end of the bias tape, sew the length of the straps closed with the stitch and turn method (page 20). If you want thinner straps over the shoulder, gradually make them narrower toward the ends. Leave the center of the bias tape open to be applied to the front of the bodice.

6 Center the tape on the front and sew the tape as if it were a waistband, using the stitch in the ditch method, from one top point of the bust around the front to the other top point of the bust. Without twisting the straps, pin them to the back as marked on the pattern, and try the top on. Adjust the lengths of the straps and tack down at the back where indicated on the pattern. Make a tiny dart in the bias tape edging at the bottom of the front V.

7 Measure and cut 6 strips of fabric the length from hem to hem over the shoulder. Be sure to cut the strips long enough; you can always snip off the extra later. There is no need to finish the edges of these strips. Lay the strips right side up on the outside of the garment; attach them by topstitching through the middle of the strip up the front, leaving the shoulder section loose, and then stitching the rest of the strip down the back. Layer the 3 strips from each side on the shoulder and tack to the spaghetti strap, making sure the center front straps are on top. Refer to above illustration for strap pattern and fabric.

Finishing Touches

8 Hand-sew a variety of small beads down the center of the 2 center front strips, from the hem to the tacking on the shoulder strap.

This lightweight long dress gives you the impression of floating through space as you walk. The added bottom flounce accents the feeling. All you need is a slight wind blowing your skirt and you will be hooked.

SKILL LEVEL   INTERMEDIATE

MATERIALS

3 yd (2.7m) fabric with pattern along the selvage (self)

1³/₄ yd (1.6m) coordinating fabric for bottom flounce (combo 1)

¹/₄ yd (23cm) silk satin in a contrasting color (combo 2)

2 yd (1.8m) charmeuse for lining

¹/₄ yd (23cm) fusible interfacing

Matching thread

15" (38cm) zipper

¹/₂ yd (45.5cm) of ¹/₄" (6mm) elastic

1 hook and eye

seam allowances

¹/₂" (13mm) for the side seams; ³/₈" (9.5mm) for all others

1   Select the pattern size according to your bust measurement. To change the length within 2" (5cm), you can add or deduct from the skirt bottom. But if the change is more than 2" (5cm), adjust the length from the seam of the skirt top to retain the design proportion. Remember to also adjust the bottom part to match the seam at the bottom of the bust. Lay out the pattern pieces on the corresponding fabrics, fitting them on the fabric however works for you, and cut. Don't forget to watch the grain lines.

2   Press fusible interfacing to the front neck band (6) and neck band extension (7).

3   Make piping for two shoulder straps (2) using the stitch and turn method (page 20). Also make ¹/₂" (13mm) double-fold bias tape from the self fabric.

4   With right sides together, sew a front neck band (6) to each front bust piece (1). Press the band flat over the seam allowance and topstitch close to the band's sewn edge. With right sides together, sew the bust cup lining (8) to the bust cup along the center front edge. Press wrong sides together. On the band, topstitch very close to the front center edge. Baste the armhole side and the bottom of the bust cup and bust cup lining together. Use the basting

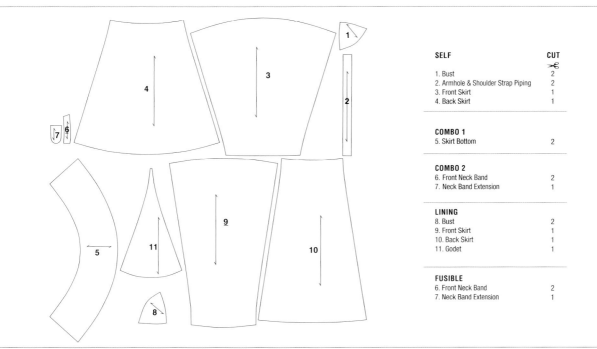

SELF	CUT
	✂
1. Bust	2
2. Armhole & Shoulder Strap Piping	2
3. Front Skirt	1
4. Back Skirt	1
COMBO 1	
5. Skirt Bottom	2
COMBO 2	
6. Front Neck Band	2
7. Neck Band Extension	1
LINING	
8. Bust	2
9. Front Skirt	1
10. Back Skirt	1
11. Godet	1
FUSIBLE	
6. Front Neck Band	2
7. Neck Band Extension	1

thread on the bottom edge as a gathering thread. Tack the straps to the top point of each bust cup, with the strap pointing down and its end flush with the edge of the bust. Finish the armhole side of the cup edge with the double-fold bias tape. The strap should be on the inside. Fold the strap up and tack it to the bias tape.

5 Turn under the contrasting center extension piece (7) and topstitch to the center top of the skirt front (3).

6 Using your favorite method or following the package directions, put the zipper in the left side seam of the front (3) and back (4) skirt pieces. Finish sewing the left seam and sew the front and back right side seam together.

7 Sew the right and left side seams of the skirt bottom (5) together. Finish with a very narrow hem. Sew the skirt bottom to the bottom of the skirt, matching the side seams and the back and front center points. Hint: Pin the skirt bottom in place. There should not be any gathers; the seam should lay flat. Make any adjustments necessary in the side seams.

8 Sew the skirt lining's right-hand side seam together (9). Sew the godet (11) into the left side seam. Finish sewing the left seam. Finish the lining with a very narrow hem.

9 Baste the bust cups to the skirt front (3), adjusting the gathers under the cups to fit.

10 With the right side of the skirt to the right side of the lining, sew the skirt lining to the skirt around the top. Understitch the front only. Turn the garment right side out. With wrong sides together, sew a casing line on the back only ¼" (6mm) from the top, leaving the ends open to insert the elastic; stitch the elastic ends to the casing to secure. Remove ½" (13mm) of stitches in two places on the back lining where the straps will attach. Insert the ends of the straps and restitch the openings very close to the top edge. Hint: Try the dress on and have a friend pin the straps where you want them.

Finishing Touches

11 Slip stitch the lining to the zipper tape.

12 Sew a hook and eye on the inside of the waist edge above the zipper.

13 With sewing thread, crochet a chain about 2" (5cm) long. Attach one end at the bottom hem of the lining on the right-hand seam line where the skirt meets the flounce. Attach the other end to the seam allowance of the dress. This will help to keep the lining from sliding around.

LOVE IN THE AFTERNOON

PAGE 134

For this dress, select a cotton with stripes that run along the grain and are varied in width, if possible. The trim on the bust is cut along the grain from one of the stripes rather than on the bias. Choose a print with a stripe wide enough to yield four pieces cut on the straight grain of the fabric, or find another fabric to use that either matches or contrasts with the stripes. This dress is lined with the same fabric.

SKILL LEVEL   INTERMEDIATE

MATERIALS

2 yd (1.8m) striped cotton

1/2 yd (45.5cm) fusible interfacing

Thread to contrast trim on bust and to match self fabric

15" (38cm) zipper

1 hook and eye

seam allowances

1/2" (13mm) for the side seams; 3/8" (9.5mm) for all others

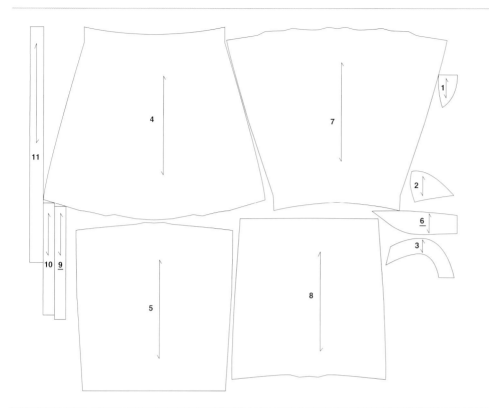

SELF	CUT ✂
1. Center Bust	4
2. Side Bust	4
3. Bust Band	4
4. Front Skirt	1
5. Front Skirt Lining	1
6. Back Body	4
7. Back Skirt	1
8. Back Skirt Lining	1
9. Right Center Shoulder Strap	1
10. Right Side/Left Shoulder Strap	2
11. Origami Strap	1

FUSIBLE	
1. Center Bust	4
2. Side Bust	4
3. Bust Band	4
6. Back Body	4

1   Select the pattern size according to your bust measurement. Lay out and cut the pattern pieces, fitting them on the fabric however works for you, and cut. Don't forget to watch the grain lines.

2   Press fusible interfacing to the bust pieces (1, 2, 3) and the back body (6).

3   Sew the 3 straps (9, 10) into tubes using the stitch and turn method (page 20). Note: 2 straps go on the right side, and 1 strap, covered with pleated trim (11), goes on the left side. Finish both edges of the strap trim (11) with rolled hems. Pin the pleats in place and topstitch the trim to the left strap down the center. **(A)**

4   Embellish the bust band (3) with 4 evenly spaced rows of very narrow zigzag stitches about ¼" (6mm) apart, parallel to the curved edges of the piece.

5   Sew the center bust (1) and the side bust (2) together, then clip the curved seam allowance. Topstitch very close to the seam line on both sides of the seam. Sew the bust cup (1, 2) to the bust band (3). Clip the curved seam allowance. Understitch.

6   Repeat step 5 with the bust lining pieces (1, 2, 3).

7   Baste the straps in place on the top edge of the bust band where indicated. Be sure that the right (public) side of the left strap trim is facing the right side of the bust cup, and the strap is pointing down with its end flush with the edge of the bust. With right sides together, stitch the bust and bust lining pieces together. Clip the curves and press to the right side.

8   Baste the pleats in place on the skirt front (4). Sew the skirt front (4) to the bust cup for about 2" (5cm) on the left side.

9   Sew the back skirt lining (8) to the back body (6). You will have two separate back body pieces (6): one left and one right. Leave openings for the straps where indicated. Clip the curves. Turn and press flat. Insert both straps between the back body lining and the back body where indicated (making sure the right (public) side of the trim on the left strap faces out on the outer body (public) side). Pin or baste. Topstitch close to the top edge on both pieces.

A

B

10 Baste the back body pieces together, overlapping as indicated. **(B)**

11 Baste the pleats in place on the skirt back (7). Sew the skirt back to the back body for about 2" (5cm) on the left side.

12 Baste the pleats on the front (5) and back (8) skirt linings. Sew the top of the front lining to front skirt lining for about 2" (5cm) on the left side. Repeat with the back lining and back skirt lining pieces. Remove all basting stitches.

Finishing Touches

13 Using your favorite method or following the directions on the package, put the zipper in the left side seam, matching the stripes on the front and back. Be careful not to get the lining caught in the seam. Finish sewing the left seam, then sew the right side seam together, again matching the stripes. Sew the right lining side seam together, matching the stripes. Sew the left seam of the lining together, leaving an opening for the zipper.

14 With right sides of the skirt back and front together, sew the body, body lining, skirt, and skirt lining together, beginning where the seams ended 2" (5cm) from the zipper.

15 Finish the lining with a very narrow double-fold hem. If at all possible, hem the skirt in such a way that the hem stitching runs along the middle of a horizontal stripe.

16 Slip stitch the lining to the zipper opening.

17 Sew the hook and eye just above the top of the zipper.

18 With thread, crochet a chain about 2" (5cm) long. Attach one end at the bottom hem of the lining on the right-hand seam line. Attach the other end to the seam allowance of the skirt. This will help to keep the lining from sliding around.

Here is a great sundress that can also be sexy in the light of the moon. These spaghetti straps have the added twist of not going down the back, but around the neck—the front and back straps intersect. The shoulder strap and front bodice pieces twist and turn in an unexpected way.

SKILL LEVEL ADVANCED

MATERIALS

2 yd (1.8m) silk and Lycra–blend charmeuse

1¹/₂ yd (1.4m) soft lining fabric

¹/₂ yd (45.5cm) fusible interfacing

Matching thread

15" (38cm) invisible zipper

¹/₄ yard (22cm) of ¹/₄" (6mm) elastic

1 hook and eye

seam allowances

¹/₂" (13mm) for the side seams; ³/₈" (9.5mm) for all others

1 Select the pattern size according to your bust measurement. Lay out the pattern pieces, fitting them on the fabric however works for you, and cut. Don't forget to watch the grain lines.

2 Press interfacing to the front bust cup (1), front and back waistband facing (5, 9), and back chest (10). On the bottom edge of the bust cup pieces, sew a gathering stitch.

3 Make 4 straps (11, 15) using the stitch and turn method (page 20). Twist each strap separately and then twist 2 of the same length together. Sew the straps together by stitching down the middle of the twisted straps, beginning and ending about 2" (5cm) from the end for the front strap; sew to the ends on the back strap.

4 Baste the 2 ends of the front strap (11) to the right bust where indicated, with the strap pointing down and its ends flush with the edge of the top of the bust piece (1). Sew the other ends of the front strap to the left front bust cup (1); the front strap will go around the back neck from bust top to bust top. Sew the cup linings to the cups. Understitch.

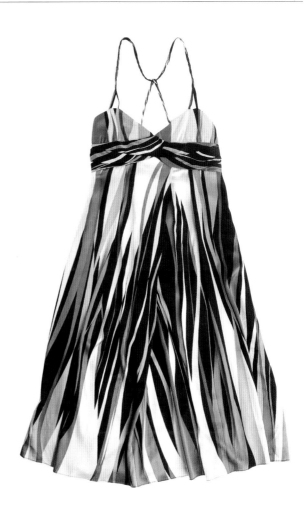

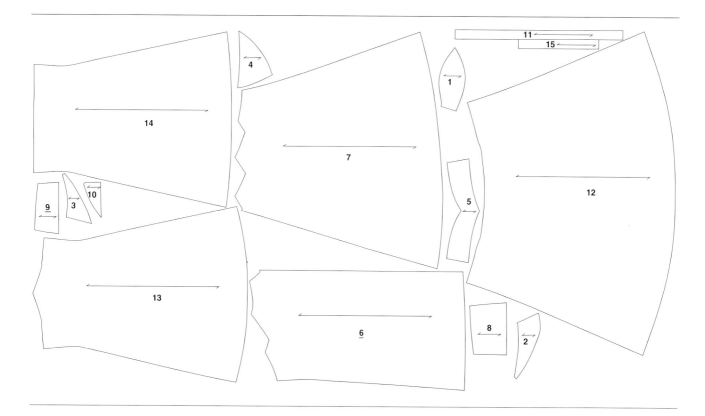

5 Sew the front right bust cup under (2) to front empire waist band (4). Repeat with pieces 3 and 4. Be careful to keep the right side of the fabric together when you sew to assure that you end up with a right and left side empire waist band. Sew the front center seam together. Sew a line of gathering stitches on the side edges of the empire waist band.

6 With right sides together, sew the completed front empire waist band to the right and left cups. Be sure to take in a few small gathers on the bottom of the cup (1). Sew the empire waist band facing (5) to the cup facings. Be very careful when pivoting where the cups come together. You may want to hand baste these pieces together first to get a perfect point.

7 With right sides together, sew the center seam of the back empire waist (8) together. Repeat with the back empire waist facing (9). Sew the back chest lining pieces (10) to the back chest pieces (10) along the top edge. With right sides together, baste the back chest pieces (10) to the top of the back empire waist band. Where the point of piece 10 meets 8, baste the ends of the back strap. The back strap loops through the front strap. (See illustration **(A)** for placement.)

8 Sew the back empire waist band lining (9) to the back chest lining, the back strap, the top of the middle of the back empire waist band, the back strap, and the back chest lining.

9 Leaving the left seam open, with right sides together, pin the right seam front and back waist band together, matching the seam where the linings meet.

10 With wrong sides together, topstitch ¼" (6mm) from side seam to side seam across the top of the back empire waist. On the inside between the back strap ends, make a tiny slit in the lining between the top edge and the topstitching. Insert elastic between in the casing. Slip stitch closed, catching the ends of the elastic.

11 Sewing only through the outside of the garment and not through the lining, run a gathering stitch in the ditch of the center back seam of the waistband, and one line of basting stitches on each side and parallel to the center seam, starting at the point where the back strap and back chest piece meet.

SELF	CUT ✂
1. Front Bust Cup	4
2. Front Right Bust Cup Under Piece	1
3. Front Left Bust Cup Under Piece	1
4. Front Empire Waist Band	2
5. Front Empire Waist Band Facing	1
6. Front Right Skirt	1
7. Front Left Skirt	1
8. Back Waistband	2
9. Back Waistband Facing	2
10. Back Chest	4
11. Front Shoulder Strap	2
12. Back Skirt	1
15. Back Shoulder Strap	2

LINING	
13. Front Lining	1
14. Back Lining	1

FUSIBLE	
1. Front Bust Cup	4
5. Front Empire Waist Band Facing	1
9. Back Waistband Facing	2
10. Back Chest	4

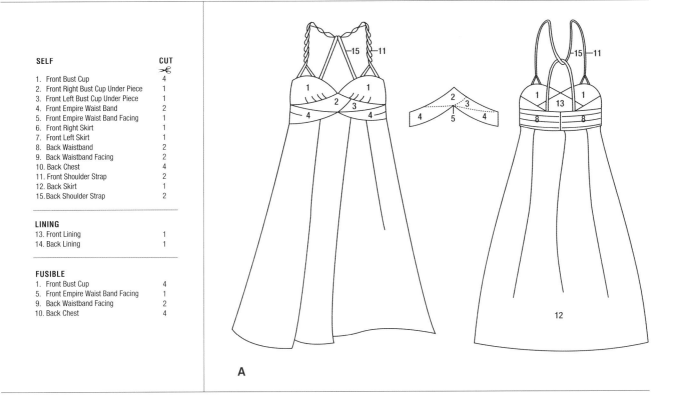

A

12 Sew the right (6) and left (7) front skirt pieces together. Leaving an opening for the zipper in the left side seam, sew the front and back skirt (12) pieces together. Finish the skirt with a rolled or very narrow hem. Baste the pleats in the direction indicated on the pattern.

13 Sew darts where indicated on the skirt lining pieces (13, 14). Leaving an opening for the zipper in the left side seam, sew the front and back skirt lining pieces together.

14 With right sides together, sew the skirt to the top, matching side seams, darts, pleats, and center front point. This becomes an empire waist line. With wrong sides together, and using the stitch in the ditch method (page 16), sew through this empire waist line seam, being careful to catch the lining in the seamline as well.

15 Gather all the lines of gathering stitches on the empire waist band. There should be 2 side seams and 3 back lines. Gather the waist band at these points so they fit the lining pieces, and topstitch the band to the lining.

16 Using your favorite method or following the directions on the package, put the zipper in the left side seam.

Finishing Touches
17 Slip stitch the lining to the zipper tape.

18 Sew the hook and eye at the top of the zipper.

17 Allow the dress to hang for a few days. Trim the skirt lining ½" (13mm) shorter than the skirt. Finish the lining with a very narrow hem.

18 With thread, crochet one or two chains each about 2" (5cm) long. Attach one end at the bottom hem of the lining on the right-hand seam line. Attach the other end to the seam allowance of the skirt. This will help to keep the lining from sliding around.

These spaghetti straps are as close to angel-hair pasta as you can get. Since the tube is so skinny, there is a trick to turning them right side out. First, make the tube as usual with the stitch and turn method, and attach a piece of string to one end of the tube. Using a blunt-end needle, thread the string back through the tube and pull the string until the tube is right side out.

Looking for a larger bubble? It's simple: Double or triple the size of the pleats! Just cut the paper front pattern piece along the pleating marks and spread the piece out, making the pleats as wide as you want. Tape the pattern pieces together with extra paper and use it as your new pattern. Don't forget to mark the pleating lines on the new pattern. Now you have a different-size bubble without changing the size of the lining!

SKILL LEVEL EASY

MATERIALS

1 yd (91cm) silk-and-wool double-knit lace (self)

$1/2$ yd (45.5cm) silk-and-wool double knit (combo)

1 yd (91cm) double knit for lining

$1/4$ yd (23cm) fusible interfacing

Matching thread

$1^1/2$ yd (1.4m) of $1/4$" (6mm) elastic

Three $5/8$" (16mm) buttons

seam allowances

$1/2$" (13mm) for the side seams; $3/8$" (9.5mm) for all others

1 Select the pattern size according to your bust measurement. If you are not using knit fabric for this project, you might want to make one size larger. Lay out the pattern pieces, fitting them on the fabric however works for you, and cut. Don't forget to watch the grain lines.

2 Press fusible interfacing (3, 4, 5) to the combo pieces.

3 Make two spaghetti straps (6) using the stitch and turn method (page 20).

4 Sew the bust side (3) to the bust center (4). Sew the bust front and back yoke (5) side seams together. Repeat with the lining pieces. Baste the straps to the front bust points and to the yoke back where indicated on the pattern. With right sides together, sew the top edge of the yoke and yoke lining together, being careful to catch the straps in the seam. Clip and trim curves. Understitch.

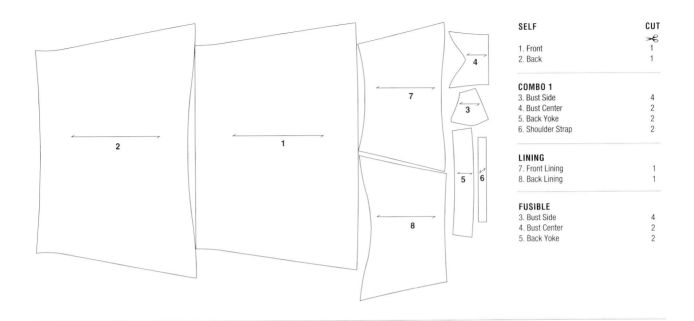

SELF	CUT ✂
1. Front	1
2. Back	1

COMBO 1	
3. Bust Side	4
4. Bust Center	2
5. Back Yoke	2
6. Shoulder Strap	2

LINING	
7. Front Lining	1
8. Back Lining	1

FUSIBLE	
3. Bust Side	4
4. Bust Center	2
5. Back Yoke	2

5 Sew the front (1) and the back (2) side seams together. Fold the top edge to the inside on the fold line indicated on the pattern. Pin the tucks in place. Adjust as needed to fit the yoke. Be sure that a fold line of the center tuck falls on the center of the front. Baste the pleats 1" (2.5cm) down from their top edge. Sew a basting stitch along the bottom edge of the garment on each side of the side seams where indicated.

6 Sew the side seams of the front (7) and back (8) lining together. With right sides together, sew the bottom edge of the lining to the bottom edge of garment, adjusting the gathers to fit. Press the seam allowance toward the lining. Sew a casing line ¼" (6mm) above the seam line. Insert a 12 (13, 14, 15, 16)" (30.5 [33, 35.5, 38, 40.5]cm) length of elastic into the casing just between the marks for gathering at each side. You will have to make a slit on the inside of the casing to get the elastic through. Tack the slit closed when you tack the elastic down at each end.

7 With right sides together, sew the lining to the yoke. Press the seam allowance toward the lining. Sew a casing line ¼" (6mm) below the seam line. Starting at a seam line, insert a length of elastic into the casing. Stitch the ends of the elastic together and stitch the opening closed. Adjust the fabric around the elastic so that there are less gathers in the back and closer gathers under the bust. Turn the garment right side out.

8 Pin the yoke to the front and back (1, 2). The wrong side of the front and back will be against the right side of the yoke. Starting from the left side seam, pin ¼" (6mm) from the top edge of the yoke and through the pleat basting line on the back. When you get to the right-hand side seam, pin the yoke line indicated on the pattern to the basting line on the front of the garment. Hint: Pin as if stitching in the ditch. You are making another elastic casing that goes from side seam to side seam around the back. Starting on the left side seam, topstitch the back yoke (5) to the back (2) and the yoke front to the front (1).

Finishing Touches

9 Open the casing on the left and right side seams. Insert the elastic in the back casing. Tack the opening closed as you tack the elastic ends at the side seams.

10 Sew 3 buttons on the front center fold where indicated.

11 Invisibly tack a few of the front pleats to the yoke to keep the pleats from flopping over.

READ BETWEEN THE LINES

The spaghetti straps in this fun top are actually more like rigatoni. There is a twist to the construction: The straps are cut all in one piece with the bust. If this doesn't work for you, or if you want different colored straps, make them separately and then attach them as you sew the lining to the bra top.

SKILL LEVEL INTERMEDIATE

MATERIALS

1 yd (91cm) solid-colored silk-and-cotton fabric (self)

½ yd (45.5cm) cotton stripe (combo)

Matching thread

⅛ yard (11cm) of ¼" (6mm) elastic

seam allowances

½" (13mm) for the side seams; ⅜" (9.5mm) for all others

1 Select the pattern size according to your bust measurement. Lay out the pattern pieces, fitting them on the fabric however works for you, and cut. Don't forget to watch the grain lines.

2 Sew stay stitches at the V where the two straps separate on both the bust and the bust lining (1). With right sides together, sew the lining and the bust and straps together, making sure to sew around the V between the parts of the straps. Clip to the V. Clip the seam allowances. Reinforce the back seam on the curve and trim close to the stitching. Understitch the curve. Turn the top to the right side. Twist each part of each strap separately and then twist both parts of each strap together. By twisting them looser or tighter, you can adjust strap length. Baste the ends to keep the straps from untwisting.

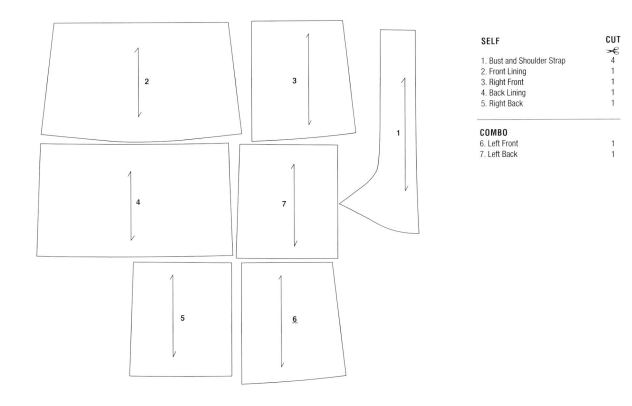

SELF	CUT
1. Bust and Shoulder Strap	4
2. Front Lining	1
3. Right Front	1
4. Back Lining	1
5. Right Back	1
COMBO	
6. Left Front	1
7. Left Back	1

3 Sew a basting thread under the cup section of the bra top. Gather slightly between the marks indicated.

4 Sew the left front (6) to the left back (7) at the side seam. Repeat with the right front (3) and the right back (5). Sew the front (2) and back (4) lining side seams together. Finish the lining hem and the blouse hem separately, each with a very narrow hem.

5 Sew a gathering thread ⅜" (9.5mm) from the top edge of the blouse front and the blouse front lining. With right sides together, pin the bust to the skirt, matching the center and back marks, adjusting the gathers in the front, and inserting the back end of the straps into the seam. With right sides together, sew the skirt lining to the skirt at the bust seam, matching seams and markings. The bust and the back straps will be sandwiched between the skirt and the skirt lining. Understitch the seam only under the bust pieces.

Finishing Touches

6 Along the top edge of the skirt back, make a ¼" (6mm) casing. From the inside, cut a slit in the casing to thread the elastic through. Tack the slits closed when tacking the elastic ends down at the side seams.

TWINKLE'S LITTLE BLACK BOOK OF SEWING RESOURCES

Most of the fabric used in this book is available for purchase at www.twinklebywenlan.com. Of course, you may want to make your own selection of fabric, too! In this section you will find suggestions for leading fabric stores to visit in person or online.

New York

The New York City Garment District, also known as the Chelsea Garment District, is located in a prime location in Manhattan between Fifth and Ninth Avenues from Thirty-Fourth to Forty-Second Street. It's home to a high concentration of garment and fabric manufacturers, especially along Sixth and Seventh Avenues, making it easy to visit many vendors without much travel time.

Fabric

Ayazmoon Fabric
214 W. 39th St.
New York, NY 10018
212-869-3315

B&J Fabrics
525 Seventh Ave., Second Floor
New York, NY 10018
212-354-8150
www.bandjfabrics.com

The City Quilter
133 W. 25th St.
New York, NY 10001
212-807-0390
www.cityquilter.com

J & O Fabrics
9401 Route 130
Pennsauken, NJ 08110
856-663-2121
www.jandofabrics.com

Kiitos Marimekko
1262 Third Ave.
New York, NY 10021
800-527-0624
212-628-8400
www.kiitosmarimekko.com

Mood Fabrics
225 W. 37th St., Third Floor
New York, NY 10018
212-730-5003
www.moodfabric.com

NY Elegant Fabrics
222 W. 40th St.
New York, NY 10018
212-302-4980
www.nyelegantfabrics.com

Paron Fabrics
Paron West/Paron Annex
206 W. 40th St.
New York, NY 10018
212-768-3266
www.paronfabrics.com

Spandex House
263 W. 38th St., Third Floor
New York, NY 10018
212-354-6711
www.spandexhouse.com

Trims & Notions

M&J Trimming
1008 Sixth Ave.
New York, NY 10018
212-391-6200
www.mjtrim.com

Jewelry Making & Beading Supplies

B & B Button & Trim
263 W. 38th St., 15th Floor
New York, NY 10018
212-631-0067

Magic Trim, Inc.
261 W. 35th St., #605
New York, NY 10001
212-465-8490

Remarkable Buttons
242 W. 36th St.
New York, NY 10018
212-810-4050
www.remarkablebutton.com

Toho Shoji
990 Sixth Ave.
New York, NY 10018
212-868-7465 or 212-868-7466
www.tohoshoji-ny.com

Atlanta

Fabric, Trims, & Notions

Atlanta Fabric
3267 Buford Hwy. NE, #730A
Atlanta, GA 30329
404-633-3313

Gail K. Fabrics
2216 Cheshire Bridge Rd. NE
Atlanta, GA 30324
404-982-0366
www.gailkfabricsinc.com

Chicago

Fabric

Fishman's Fabrics
1101 S. Desplaines St.
Chicago, IL 60607
312-922-7250
www.fishmansfabrics.com

Vogue Fabrics
623–627 W. Roosevelt Rd.
Chicago, IL 60607
312-829-2505
www.voguefabricsstore.com

Trims & Notions

Chicago Fabric Yarn & Button Sales
314 W. Adams St.
Chicago, IL 60606
312-726-5688

Dallas

Fabric, Trims, & Notions

Golden D'or Fabric Outlet
10797 Harry Hines Blvd.
Dallas, TX 75220
214-351-2339
www.goldendoroutlet.com

Sari Palace
100 S. Central Expy.,
Suite 33
Richardson, TX 75080
972-680-8238

Denver

Fabric, Trims, & Notions

Denver Fabric
2777 W. Belleview Ave.
Littleton, CO 80123
303-730-2777
www.denverfabrics.com

Heritage Home Fabrics and More
5550 E. Evans Ave.
Denver, CO 80222
303-758-0566
www.heritagefabrics.com

Los Angeles

Fabric, Trims, & Notions

California Market Center
110 E. Ninth St., Suite A727
Los Angeles, CA 90079
213-630-3600
www.californiamarketcenter
.com

These vendors are worth a visit at the California Market Center:

Calamo Silk
110 E. Ninth St., Suite B1271
Los Angeles, CA 90079
213-622-3800
www.calamosilk.com

Happy Fabric
820 Maple Ave.
Los Angeles, CA 90014
213-489-7781

Malibu Textiles, Inc.
2833 Leonis Blvd.,
Suite 101–102
Vernon, CA 90058
213-891-1450
www.malibutextiles.com

Murano, Inc.
821 Santee St., Suite M-52
Los Angeles, CA 90014
213-891-9144
www.muranoinc.com

Miami

Fabric, Trims, & Notions

Trim-Rite Trimming & Lace
2120 NW 23rd Ave.
Miami, FL 33142
305-633-7577

Online Stores

Alexander Henry Fabrics, Inc.
www.ahfabrics.com

Discount Fabric
www.discountfabric.com

IKEA
www.ikea.com

Reprodepot
www.reprodepot.com

Trim Fabric
www.trimfabric.com

INDEX

HOW TO MAKE
THE PATTERNS

Patterns for each garment come in five sizes—0, 4, 8, 12, and 16—on the enclosed disc. The patterns are in PDF and Adobe Illustrator format and can be printed on 8½" x 11" (21.5cm x 28cm) sheets on your home printer. Tape the sheets together, matching the numbers on each corner, and then cut out the pattern pieces. The clear markings on the patterns make taping and cutting them easy to manage from home.

The PDF patterns are viewable using Adobe Reader, available for download free of charge at http://get.adobe.com/reader/

The Illustrator patterns are viewable using Adobe Illustrator, which is available for purchase at http://www.adobe.com/products/illustrator/